Edge of Conflict

God Bless You!
In His Name!
Miriam Harry
Taylor

Deltawhake - July '96
Family Conf.

EDGE
OF
CONFLICT

THE STORY OF
HARRY AND MIRIAM TAYLOR

Harry and Miriam Taylor

Christian Publications
CAMP HILL, PENNSYLVANIA

Christian Publications
3825 Hartzdale Drive, Camp Hill, PA 17011

The mark of ✝ *vibrant faith*

ISBN 0-87509-511-9
LOC Catalog Card Number: 93-70744
© 1993 by Christian Publications
All rights reserved
Printed in the United States of America

93 94 95 96 97 5 4 3 2 1

Cover Illustration © 1993, Karl Foster

The chronicles of the camp experiences are based on our memories, on loose-leaf notes kept during
those years and reference to the following books:

Crouter, Natalie. *Forbidden Diary.* New York: Burt Franklin and Co., 1980.
Hind, R. Renton. *Spirits Unbroken.* San Francisco: John Howell, 1946.
Hyland, Judy. *In the Shadow of the Rising Sun.* Minneapolis, MN: Augsburg Publishing House, 1984.
Miles, Fern Harrington. *Captive Community.* Jefferson City, TN: Mosey Creek Press, 1987.
Yerger, Esther. *Ambassadors in Bonds.* E. Stroudsburg, PA: Pinebrook Book Club, 1946.

Other sources:
Johnston, Russ with Maureen Rank. *God Can Make It Happen.* Wheaton, IL: Victor Books, 1976.
Snyder, Louis L. *Historical Guide to World War II.* Westport, CT: Greenwood Press, 1982.
Tozer, A.W. *Renewed Day by Day.* Camp Hill, PA: Christian Publications, Inc., 1980.

Contents

Appreciation

This book is dedicated to the host of prayer warriors who support missionary enterprise with whole-hearted devotion and sacrifice for Christ and His Kingdom! When on furlough from the mission field we spoke in missionary conferences in many states, in Canada, in Australia and New Zealand. You in the churches entertained us in your homes, provided for us, made us feel welcome. Furlough over. You sent us back to the mission field equipping us with an outfit, supporting us with your love, encouraging us by your interest, fortifying us with your prayers. God bless you each one!

Janice Kropp, our daughter in Tokyo, Japan, for planting the seeds for writing *Edge of Conflict*.
Marilynne Foster, of Christian Publications, for watering the seeds. She has counseled us by telephone and in person.
Grace Fry of Upland, Indiana, for helping to purchase a word processor for typing the initial copies of the manuscript.
Judith Esther Reitz, our daughter, in Brooklyn, New York, for lovingly applying her newly acquired skills in word processing to this project; for her time and helpful suggestions.
Donald M. Taylor, our son in Binghamton, New

York, for his help with information and the performing of many tasks so as to free us to write.

Ping Moy, of Christ's Community Church in Brooklyn, New York, for giving up his computer and software for the typing of the final manuscript.

Joe Vargas, also of Christ's Community Church for donating reams of computer paper.

Fern Harrington Miles for her sketches of the concentration camp scenes in the Philippines. She, too, lived through the experience.

Part I

America: Conditioning for the Conflict

The LORD your God is with you,
he is mighty to save.
He will take great delight in you.
(Zephaniah 3:17a)

1

"... And What Is Too Hard for You"

(Miriam)

It was the spring of 1966. I was tired. We had just completed 28 years of ministry abroad and had been back in the States only six months. I was still recovering from allergies that had developed in Cambodia as a result of the intense heat, humidity, mold, mildew and rice pollen.

After having been forced out of Cambodia due to the political developments in Indochina, we had been requested by our Mission board to transfer to Lebanon. It was too fast for me, the situation was too unpredictable. I needed a little time. I was not ready to face another term on a mission field I knew firsthand to be a difficult one.

Not only that. Our youngest daughter, Judy, was soon to graduate from college and was considering marriage. Didn't I have any rights as a mother? We had not attended the graduations of any of our three children either from high school or college. We had invested heavily in missionary involvement.

Surely we had done our part, at least for a while.

About that time, my husband and I were asked to speak at an interfaith women's meeting at the Jersey City Mission in New Jersey. Two hundred and fifty women gathered to hear about Cambodia.

After the opening song, one of the local women gave a brief devotional. As she read from Deuteronomy—God's message to the children of Israel through Moses—my wandering thoughts jerked to attention.

"You have been in this mount long enough," she read. We were living at Nyack, New York, often called the "mount of prayer and blessing."

"Break camp and advance—to Lebanon," the Lord said again through His Word. And "bring Me any case too hard for you."

I was beginning to feel uncomfortable. The speaker's intent was obvious—to challenge the women to move ahead in their walk with God, to know Him in deeper ways. What she did not realize was that her message was custom-made by the Holy Spirit for a reluctant missionary!

A few days later, some friends handed us the keys to their cottage on the Jersey shore and said, "Why don't you go down to the ocean for a rest?"

A rest was what I needed—some time to be alone, to be quiet, to think, to pray, to align my will with God's will. I wanted God's will, but to make His thoughts my thoughts and His way my way sometimes took a little while.

Judy and Harry and I arrived at the shore on a hot, clear day. From the cottage we could see the waves rolling onto the beach. We had come to relax, to meditate and to pray about the critical decision we were about to make.

The surf looked inviting. As we stepped into the water, I noticed that Harry was still wearing his sunglasses.

"Honey," I called, "you have your sunglasses on!"

"Don't worry," he replied. "I'll be careful."

"But I paid a lot for those glasses," I persisted.

My warnings went unheeded.

The breakers were rolling in, splashing the cool water up our legs and sifting the sand through our toes as they clutched for solid footing.

Suddenly, at an unguarded moment, a big wave hit Harry, throwing him into the churning water. Somersaulting head over heels, he finally came up spitting and sputtering. And the glasses? They were gone.

Gone!

Annoyed, I stood there silently staring at the horizon. I felt like saying, "I told you so," but I didn't want to press the point. At least not right then. I knew that Harry would already be sorry he had not listened.

He decided to hunt for them. Whether to make me feel better or whether he actually thought he had one chance in a million of finding them, I didn't know. I couldn't believe he would tackle such an impossible task.

I could see the waves rolling over his head, the undertow tugging at his feet, debris washing by him into the shore and out again. He was looking, looking, trying to figure out where the glasses might be.

Then, suddenly, I saw him take a quick dive. He must have seen something that looked familiar. Then, momentarily, he surfaced, only sand slipping through his clenched fists.

"I saw them," he called with satisfaction, "but they were traveling so fast I couldn't grab them. They might be headed for Europe—or even Lebanon, for all I know."

Lebanon. With the tide lapping at my toes, I was deep in thought, about to dream up something quite impossible of my own.

"Lord," I whispered out loud, "if you want us, really want us, to go to Lebanon, let Harry come up with those glasses!"

Finding a needle in a haystack is a tough assignment, but to have the rough Atlantic give up a pair of sunglasses? That would indeed be a miracle!

Harry continued his search. With time to survey the surf, could he now better judge its speed and direction? How far would the glasses have traveled? Would they be farther out or farther in?

Harry dove into the surf again. As he broke up through the waves, he raised one hand in the air. He had the glasses!

"Oh, no," I cried unvolitionally.

Judy turned to me.

"Mother," she said softly, "you'd better go to Lebanon."

2

"Break Camp and Advance"

(Miriam)

Actually, the mission field had always been my home. I was just eight years old when my parents sailed for the Near East in 1923. When I was born, George and Lola Breaden were not even believers. Oh yes, they attended church regularly, they sang in the choir and they even taught Sunday school. But they did not know Jesus Christ in a personal way. But, as God sometimes works, He managed to get their attention through a life and death situation that involved someone very special to them—me.

I was two years old, sick in bed with a very high fever.

"There's nothing more I can do for your little girl," the doctor said as he picked up his bag and turned away from the bed. As he walked out the front door of our home on Martin Street in Greenville, Ohio, a neighbor, Florence Moore, came in the back door.

"I heard your little Miriam was sick and I've come to pray for her," Florence offered. Although somewhat taken aback, Mother and Dad were open to any suggestion that would make their daughter well. To their amazement, God answered Florence's prayer of faith. The fever left. I got better.

At Mrs. Moore's invitation, Mother and Dad decided to attend The Christian and Missionary Alliance Church which was meeting in an upstairs room over a feed store on Broadway. There they heard their first salvation message. Their hearts were stirred and both went to the altar to ask the Lord Jesus Christ to forgive their sins and be the Master of their lives.

At the annual missionary conference of this small church my parents heard the challenge of reaching the world for Christ. Both Mother and Dad felt the call of God to become missionaries. However, they didn't dare tell each other how they felt.

Mother thought that Dad would never leave his thriving foundry business. As the oldest son of the Breaden family, he was soon to replace his father as president of the Treaty Company. At the same time, Dad figured Mother would not be willing to leave the security she enjoyed in their lovely, new home on Martin Street.

One day, Mother, no longer able to contain herself, exploded, "George, I'm called to be a missionary!"

Thrusting his arms toward heaven, Dad exclaimed, "Praise the Lord, so am I!"

Radical changes began to take place. The house on Martin Street was sold and suitcases and trunks were packed. We were on our way to Nyack, New York, where Dad had been accepted as a ministerial student at Nyack Missionary Training Institute.

The only house our little family—Mother, Dad, my younger sister, Marjorie and I—could find was a tiny servants' quarters attached to a large mansion on South Boulevard. After several months in those cramped quarters, my parents jumped at the offer to move into a larger house. We had to share it with the Sheltons, but at least the rent could be divided between two families. The extra space was especially appreciated when, during the second year at Nyack, Evelyn was born.

Grandfather Breaden did not understand the abrupt and revolutionary change in Dad's plans. He made it plain he would not help us financially, but several times during those three years of schooling Grandpa's concern got the best of him.

In those days, most missionaries went to the field single and only after language study were they permitted to get married. The George Breadens were not only married—they had three children!

Arriving in Jaffa, Palestine, Mother and Dad were assigned to Beersheba to study the language and to be in charge of the Mission station and its district.

I still remember our first trip to Jerusalem. We made the long day's trip by motorcycle—Mother, Marge and Evelyn in the sidecar, and me straddling the seat behind Dad. The Arabic Girls' School, where I was about to be left, was run by our Mission. It was located in the headquarters compound on Prophet Street. Most of my lessons were in Arabic, a language which soon became second nature to me.

After language study, my parents were transferred from Beersheba to Ma'an, near the Arabian border. In those days, Saudi Arabia was a closed country, but Dad had a deep love for those people and he hoped to eventually take the gospel to them. He felt that they had a right to hear, too.

Mother and Dad found a house in Ma'an made of mud bricks dried in the sun. The house was fine until one year, during the rainy season, one of the bedroom walls caved in. Fortunately, the compound was surrounded by high walls—impossible to climb over—so we were protected from intruders.

Within the compound was an open well. Once, when my father was on one of his several desert trips, and the date of his planned return had long passed, Mother began imagining him and those with him lying dead somewhere out in the desert. Satan began to tempt her to end her own life by throwing herself into the well. Wisely, she ordered the well sealed.

After what seemed an eternity, the men returned with remarkable stories of God's deliverance. The main reason for the delay was that the axle on the Model T Ford had broken in the desert. Their guide led them by foot to the coastal village of Tema where they were put in prison, accused of being spies. For what other reason would foreigners be wandering in the desert?

While Mother was being tempted back in Ma'an

with thoughts of suicide, Dad, and his companion, Rev. William Smalley, Sr., were experiencing unusual blessing. When one of the prison officials was taken with a high fever, Dad and Mr. Smalley, eager to be faithful witnesses for Christ, prayed for his healing. God answered miraculously and providentially.

Believing these foreigners to be superhuman, their fearful hosts put the two men on a small ship bound for Port Said where they were evicted from the country!

The men arrived home the day after Christmas. What a relief! They had been gone several months with no communication back home. Eventually someone was sent back to the desert with a spare part and the Model T was retrieved.

That same Model T served as our means of transportation to and from the Mission school that had been moved from Jerusalem to Beit-Jala near Bethlehem. At vacation times, Dad would come to get us (Marjorie was now with me). The trip was long and tedious. Fortunately the car had side curtains which protected us from the sand and wind that blew without mercy. We always took food and water with us, but the heat was suffocating.

Once we were home, the long, hard trip was soon forgotten. A big, beautiful and expensively furnished house could not have afforded more love than we enjoyed in our humble, mud brick house.

As children, we were always home for Christmas. Our little missionary family didn't have much money. Allowance cuts of 50 percent were quite common in those days. Buying gifts for each other was out of the question.

I remember one Christmas especially. We were so delighted with the gifts Mother gave us—personalized laundry bags made of khaki colored cloth with the word "Laundry" embroidered across the front.

While in Ma'an, my folks hired a houseboy/gardener named Jamael Tahan, a Muslim. When he accepted the job he made it clear that he had no intention of becoming a Christian.

Jamael settled in and learned to do his work well. He also showed considerable interest in our habits and customs, particularly our practice of meeting together every day for family devotions.

When it came time for Jamael to have a few days leave, Dad gave him a New Testament. He took it home with him, knowing that if he was going to read it, it would have to be in secret.

In the middle of the night Jamael would light a candle and read the Testament in the privacy of his own room. All went well until one night his father unexpectedly stomped into the room, snatched the Testament out of his hands and tore it to shreds. Jamael never opened his mouth. Yet, he was permitted to come back to us. When he returned he asked Dad to pray with him and Jamael became a Christian. It was a miracle!

On Jamael's next visit home, his family tried to force him to renounce his new faith, but Jamael wasn't even tempted. He had seen Christian faith in action. He now had peace in his heart. No one could take that away from him.

When his father saw that he was determined to

remain a believer, they decided to do away with him. Unknowingly, Jamael ate some poisoned food and became very sick. Suspecting he had been poisoned, he stole out of the house to a friend who was a pharmacist. The antidote administered, Jamael's life was spared. He fled to Bethlehem where he found work and later married a Christian girl.

Having completed eighth grade at the Mission school, I transferred to the British Girls' College in Jerusalem and once again lived at our Mission guest house on Prophet Street. Armenians, Arabs, Jews, Greeks, Russians and British—all were enrolled at the new school. I was the only American.

My best friend was a Russian girl, Valentina Kolikova. She lived just a block away and we had many happy times together. We would often go on Saturday excursions with other classmates. We didn't have bicycles—we had donkeys. Riding donkeyback, we visited many interesting places around Jerusalem.

One particularly interesting trip was to the Cave of Adullam (meaning refuge or retreat). Leaving the donkeys tied to a bush, we ran to explore the cave. Inching our way on our bellies past the first chamber and through a low passageway, we discovered a large inner chamber. This, we were told, was where David and his men hid from King Saul (1 Samuel 22:1).

On one of my mother's visits to the school, I asked her to help me tell Valentina about Christ. As we explained the way of salvation, Valentina opened her heart and invited Jesus in.

Not long after we returned to the States on furlough, a letter arrived from a mutual friend. "Valentina," it said, "fell off her donkey last week. She died instantly. A broken neck." My heart ached, but I was glad Mother and I had led her to Christ.

On furlough our family lived in Upland, Indiana, while Dad studied toward his master's degree at Taylor University. The two years passed quickly and it was time to return to the mission field for a second term. I, however, would stay in North America.

I'll never forget the heartache. I was only 16 years old. It would be seven years before I would see my family again. Dorothy Mae had been added to our family of five just before we came home on furlough. To think of the years of separation—seven years is a long time. And during those seven years there would be no international phone calls, no airmail letters—only boat mail.

Even though Grandfather Breaden stood beside me on the platform of the train station, I felt lonely and alone. I was to keep house for Grandpa during the summer until I entered Taylor University for my freshman year.

The train whistle blew. The belching engine inched forward.

Mother was sobbing. Everybody was crying. I could hardly catch my breath. I was waving, waving, until the train—and my family—disappeared down the tracks and out of sight.

3

The Stamp

(Miriam)

But Lord, the stamp will cost five cents and I don't have even one cent to my name! Is there any use writing a letter when I don't have a stamp to mail it?"

I was now attending Nyack Missionary Training Institute. I had transferred from Taylor University after my freshman year. And at this moment I needed a stamp to mail a letter to my parents.

Mail was slow in those days. It took a whole month for a letter to reach my folks and another month to get an answer back. *What use is it to write them about my problems?* I thought to myself. *Before I get an answer back the problem will be solved and probably forgotten. Still, they do need to hear from me. I guess I'll start the letter now and finish it when I can buy a stamp.*

It was hard to know what to write. *Why not ask them a lot of questions. I want to know about my new baby brother, John Paul, already more than two months old. I can't believe he is real! I hope I get a picture soon. And what a coincidence—he was born on my*

boyfriend's birthday—November 28th! It will be so
many years before I see him. He won't even know me.

Maybe I'll tell them about Harry Taylor coming to sit
beside me in the library. I really don't know him, but he
asked me to go with him to the Congress of Bands in
New York City on February 22nd. All the students will
be going together on the bus. In any case, I'll ask
Madge [Rigsbee] to ask her boyfriend [Frank Nagle]
to get me a little information about Harry before I have
to give him an answer tomorrow.

And what else shall I tell them? Oh yes, I'll tell them
about the kitchen crew—Evelyn Davis, Ruth Henry and
myself. Kitchen duty is long and tiresome and when I get
back to my room I just flop on the bed and my room-
mate [Carol Severn] teaches me the lessons for the next
day. Her boyfriend [George Klein] is in my Spanish
class. I carry notes back and forth between them.

It's time for Singspiration in Chapel Hall. I'll finish
this tomorrow. Hopefully I'll get a dollar in a letter—
five cents for the stamp and 95 cents left over for some-
thing else.

The song leader announced, "Faith Is the Victory." I flipped through the pages of the hymnbook
until I found the number. Lo and behold, between
the pages lay a five cent coin—the exact amount I
needed for the stamp.

After the hymn the leader said, "Each testimony
this evening will be limited to just five words." Well,
I had just found five cents, but I needed a lot more
than five words to tell the students how God had
answered my prayer. His provision of such a small
thing was an experience I will never forgot.

During my three years at Nyack many life-changing decisions had to be made. I needed counsel. So I decided to visit Professor Harold Freligh at his home on the hillside.

Professor Freligh welcomed me warmly. He was probably used to students coming with problems.

"I would like to know how to receive guidance from the Lord about His will for my life," I said. "I want to know what my life's work will be. Also, is it God's will for me to marry the young man I'm dating? He has asked me to marry him if he makes good in the ministry. I want to know what the Lord thinks about our friendship."

"The Lord will guide you step by step," Professor Freligh responded. "There are promises in God's Word that assure us He is interested in helping us: 'I will instruct you and teach you in the way you should go,' and many others. Also, along with Scripture, let me suggest two other steps to follow when you're seeking the Lord for guidance: first, tell God you sincerely want His will for your life. Then, secondly, start out in the way you think God wants you to go, whether it is a decision about your life's work or about whom you will marry.

"Look at it this way. A pilot guides a ship safely into harbor by lining up three lights one behind the other so that they become one single light. Then he knows he will be able to steer the ship in the right channel and bring it safely to shore.

"The same is true with God's children. We have three guiding lights to help us make right decisions: the peace of God in our hearts, the hand of God in our circumstances and the promises of the Word of God."

That was what I needed to hear. I got up to leave. "Thank you so much," I said. Already I was sensing the peace of God in my heart.

That was 1934. Harry Taylor and I were married September 9, 1935, and together we determined to serve the Lord in full-time ministry.

4

Empty Seats
and Angels

(Harry)

I was born in Venango, a little town in Western Pennsylvania. The first six months of my life I lived on the brink of death until nourishment could be found that agreed with me.

When I was three years old, my parents moved to Cambridge Springs, about three miles away, and bought a baking business.

In those early years I seemed to be in trouble more often than not. Playing with matches resulted in burning the roof off of the barn belonging to the bakery; an accident while playing "follow the leader" caused me to lose my front teeth; a BB gun escapade, which included shooting into the neighbor's shed through a small window, regrettably ended when the neighbor's son was hit; and skating all winter on the nearby river, pushing the odds of survival almost to the brink by skating on "rubber ice"—all appealed to my venturesome nature.

Our home in Cambridge Springs was attached to the bakery. This was good in some ways, but not in others. We always had plenty of bread and desserts, but at five o'clock in the morning I was often pulled out of bed when the assistant baker didn't show up for work. This caused me to become disenchanted with the bakery business at a very early age!

As a child I had an awesome fear of the unknown although I was at the same time enthralled by exotic sunsets, always wondering what lay beyond. I had no idea then how many exotic sunsets I would see from an assortment of distant vantage points during my life.

I was 16 when two weeks of special meetings, sponsored by all the protestant churches, were held in my hometown. Each church took turns hosting the meetings. Rev. Blackmore, head of the Erie City Mission, was the evangelist. There was a large response to the preaching each night and many, including our family, came to know Christ.

After my conversion, I adopted Joshua 1:9 as my life verse: "Have I not commanded you? Be strong and courageous. . . ." The Lord confirmed this verse to me many times during the years of missionary service.

An Alliance church was started in our community by Rev. P.R. Hyde. Impressed with the message and mission of the Alliance, my family began to attend. We young people often got together and held street meetings, witnessing to people we knew and who knew us.

When the call of God came to my heart to enter the ministry and go to Nyack, little did I realize what the Lord was working out for this young, in-experienced and often awestruck student from a small town in Western Pennsylvania.

In my class at Nyack was an attractive young woman who had come from the Near East. Her parents were missionaries with the Alliance. Obviously providence was working on my behalf, for the name Taylor was already stenciled all over her trunks and suitcases. (She was a transfer student from Taylor University!) Gradually I succeeded in convincing her that she should adopt the name Taylor as her own.

After graduation, since Miriam had no home in the States and no money, my father offered her summer employment in the family bakery. This helped her purchase what she needed for our wedding in September.

Then began the search for a ministry that would prepare us for the mission field. We soon discovered that not many churches were anxious to have a young, inexperienced, newly graduated man as their pastor. We prayed and we waited. Finally, in youthful desperation, we asked God for a church that would teach us to grow, to mature and to endure hardness for future ministry.

God answered our prayers!

We received a letter from P.R. Hyde. He had started many Alliance churches and was now interested in opening one in Norfolk, Virginia. No one seemed ready or willing to take up the challenge. He asked if we would be interested.

We had prayed. God had answered. Norfolk it would be!

Nothing was said about travel money or salary. Those were the years of the depression. We didn't worry about money. There wasn't very much money around to worry about!

With all of our possessions packed in one trunk, we bought our tickets with some wedding gift money and boarded a bus for Norfolk. There we were welcomed by Mr. and Mrs. Clifford Oakey, a most gracious couple. Bless their hearts—they gave us the guest room in their humble, over-furnished home. The only place for our belongings was under our bed. It was a good thing we had so little!

The Oakeys owned a small brick church at the corner of 39th and Elkorn. If the church grew, they said, they would give the building to the Alliance. The church had been left unpainted and unattended for years. We certainly had our work cut out for us. As to salary, it was a weekly freewill offering given by two or three couples and several children.

One day, the Oakeys informed us that they were going north for three months to visit family. Their car was no sooner out of sight than we set out to transform the house to our liking. All their extra books and unneeded (in our opinion) furniture we stacked in the Oakey's bedroom. Our plan, of course, was to have everything back in place before their scheduled return.

One day, however, we came home from out of town and found the Oakey's car in the driveway!

Summoning our courage, we walked toward the door. How would our usually whistling host greet us this time? We needn't have worried. Brother Oakey met us at the door with a broad smile and a friendly handshake. Not one word was said about the "renovations" that had taken place in his absence. And, to our amazement, we didn't have to put anything back—they had already done it!

Pastoring the little church was a struggle. Spiritual response was sparse, our existence just as sparse. We were often discouraged. The closest sister church was hours away and no one understood our situation. At the time, it seemed more than we could handle. We wondered what we should do.

Unexpectedly, I received a phone call to candidate in a church in East St. Louis, Missouri. They even offered to pay my travel expenses. That was wonderful. We weren't used to such generosity.

I accepted the invitation. It was so rewarding to minister to a sizable congregation. They told me if I decided to accept their call they would give us a livable salary and a travel expense account for our ministry.

How tempting! Could it be that now we could lay aside what appeared to be a hopeless cause and take up a new, exciting challenge? Could this be the will of God for us? I must admit I hoped so.

Arriving back in Norfolk, I told Miriam about the wonderful offer from East St. Louis. We, Harry and Miriam Taylor, were headed for bigger and better things!

While in the throes of making this important decision, we decided to drive to Washington, D.C., and talk with Brother Hyde. He, after all, should be the first to know that we were considering a move.

Completely optimistic, as always, Brother Hyde didn't wait for us to share our discouragement about the ministry in Norfolk nor the new, attractive opportunity we had received. He began to praise the Lord! He told us how thankful he was that we had accepted the Norfolk challenge. He emphasized that God had great blessings in store for us there. We prayed together and found ourselves on our way home without having said one single word about East St. Louis.

Days of agony followed. East St. Louis seemed to be the right direction. So, several weeks later, we resigned from the Norfolk church.

After the farewell service we returned to our room in the Oakey house. Since we were leaving early the next morning, we needed to finish packing.

In the midst of it all, I turned to Miriam.

"I don't feel right about leaving here," I said.

"I don't feel right, either," she replied.

We dropped everything and fell on our knees.

"Lord, is leaving a mistake? We are willing to stay. Just give us peace in our hearts. We want to make the right decision. We really do."

Just then the phone rang. It was Mrs. Moore, one of the faithful.

"On your way to Missouri in the morning, stop by our house," she said. "We have some money to help you with gas."

"We're not sure whether we're going or not," I responded hesitatingly. "In fact, we may be staying."

"Praise the Lord!" Mrs. Moore exclaimed. "We'll double the amount!"

We stayed.

Still, the growth of the church was agonizingly slow. One Sunday, early in the morning, I was sitting on the front pew praying. Tears were running down my cheeks. I was thoroughly discouraged. I had preached long enough to empty seats and angels. I wondered if it would ever be any different.

"How did I ever get into this?" I asked myself and perhaps the Lord, too. Right then, He graciously showed me the little church filled with people. It was a vision that would later be fulfilled.

The Moores, the Hevesseys, the Oakeys, the Lawrences and others doubled their efforts to help build up the congregation of that little brick church on the corner. Soon Miriam and I were able to rent our own apartment. It was meagerly furnished with one new couch and a bunch of secondhand furniture, but it was adequate. The congregation began to grow, the Lord blessed and miracles began to happen in the lives of individuals.

Before many months, the church building was given to the Alliance as the Oakeys had promised. In addition, six young people from that congregation went to Nyack Missionary Training Institute to prepare to serve Christ.

We had prayed for a church that would teach us to grow, to mature and to endure hardness for future ministry.

God had answered our prayers!

5

Under Sealed Orders

(Harry)

It was the fall of 1938. Our application for missionary service had been accepted and we were appointed to serve in Central Vietnam. Unknown to us, we were about to make a decision that would affect our lives in a most critical and decisive way.

At the time, we were considering whether to enroll at Wheaton College for further study or to go directly to Vietnam. Miriam's parents were living in Wheaton while Dad Breaden studied during their furlough. It would have been nice to be with the family for a time.

However, after much thought and prayer, we felt led to head for Vietnam. This momentous decision turned into seven long years of testing—testing in war, sickness, near starvation, extended periods of separation, and yes, even death itself.

In December of that year, Miriam and I, with our son, Don, almost two years old, sailed for France to enroll in language study. The crossing of the Atlantic was exceedingly rough. Waves washed like

liquid mountains over the deck. There were sleepless nights and anxious hours. Many passengers
stayed in their bunks for the entire crossing. Others
barely staggered into the dining hall at meal times.
The ship would roll and toss so violently that the
table settings would take to the air and crash
against the bulkhead, breaking into countless
pieces. Needless to say, we were relieved when we
finally arrived at Cherbourg, France.

Our days in France turned out to be abbreviated.
Scheduled to be there a year, we had to leave after
only eight months because war seemed imminent.
We left Paris for Marseille during the latter days of
August, 1939, to seek bookings on a ship bound for
Saigon.

Our missionary group consisted of Harold and
Agnes Dutton, Herb and Ruth Clingen, Miriam,
Don and myself. We were finally able to make
bookings on the passenger liner, *Felix Rouselle*. We
expected to sail on September 1st, but the crew
was conscripted. The same thing happened on September 2nd. We wondered if we would ever be able
to leave port.

On the third day of September, World War II
was declared and our ship finally sailed out into the
Mediterranean, blacked out, and under sealed orders.

We headed for North Africa and followed the
coastline to the Suez Canal, crossed the Indian
Ocean and finally reached Saigon, Vietnam. At last
we felt we were out of reach of the tentacles of war.

Without our knowledge, during the voyage,
Miriam and I had been reassigned from Vietnam to

Cambodia. The Clingens and Duttons were permitted to disembark in Saigon because they were to serve in Laos and Vietnam. But we were informed that Phnom Penh, Cambodia, would be our destination.

The French authorities refused to let us disembark as we lacked the necessary documents. They also took no responsibility to feed us. Thankfully, our faithful room steward managed to provide us with food during the two days it took for the Mission chairman to obtain "in transit" status for us.

How glad we were to set our feet on solid ground once again! We were driven to Phnom Penh, the capital city of Cambodia, and stayed there for a few days of orientation. The field chairman then took me by car north to Kompong Cham, a provincial capital. We were unable to find a permanent place to live in Kompong Cham, so we rented a room in The Bungalow, a typical French hotel. Miriam, Don and I stayed there for several months until we located a storefront suitable for a chapel. We moved into the apartment above it.

It was wonderful to have our own home at last, but how challenging our lifestyle became. We cooked on charcoal in the kitchen behind the chapel on the first floor. (The rest of our living quarters were upstairs!) We ironed our clothes with a charcoal iron. A five-gallon kerosene tin with an inserted shelf and an attached hinged door served as our oven when placed over the charcoal.

Our refrigerator was a little Japanese wide-mouth thermos, just big enough to hold some canned butter and ice which we bought at the local ice house.

To keep the overly proliferate ant population from sharing our bed, we balanced the four bedposts on wooden blocks placed in small containers filled with kerosene. Mosquito nets hung from each corner of the bed. Our mode of transportation was two bicycles.

It is impossible to describe the emotions of a new missionary in a foreign land, especially when war is about to engulf much of the world. With France having capitulated to Hitler, Cambodia became an orphan and was attacked by Thailand. There were frequent bombings on the border. It was rumored that fighting would soon reach our province of Kompong Cham.

Bombing in Siem Reap province had already forced Harold and Marguerite Sechrist, also first term missionaries, to come south and stay with us. Kompong Cham would logically be the next target. Miriam and I began to discuss what we should do. At the time she and Don both had the measles and menacingly high fevers.

The apartment and chapel were right across from the public market in the center of the city, a likely air raid target.

Our fears were about to be realized. It was early afternoon, siesta time, when the piercing scream of air raid sirens confirmed our worst dread. The sleepy town came alive with people fleeing for shelter. I gathered Miriam and four-year-old Don from their beds. We staggered down the concrete steps from our apartment, and, in the stifling tropical heat, made our way down the crushed stone road to a clump of kapok trees out past the edge of town. At least the leafy foliage provided shade and hid us from aerial view.

We waited on a log, with others squatting on the ground, scanning the skies and wondering what would happen next. Enemy planes never arrived, and soon, much to our relief, the all-clear siren sounded. We slowly returned home.

Border skirmishes lasted for six months. Then the French gave northern Cambodia to Thailand.

We were expecting our second child, so after the annual field conference in May at Dalat, Vietnam, Miriam and Don stayed an extra month to escape the extreme heat that comes between the dry and wet seasons in Cambodia. I returned to Kompong Cham, two days' travel time from Dalat.

Being that far apart during such uncertain times was difficult. In July, Miriam and Don came down from the mountains to Saigon and continued by bus to Phnom Penh where I was to meet them. Miriam was now five months pregnant.

On the bus heading to Phnom Penh I was suddenly smitten with an intense headache and high fever. Thinking it might be heat stroke, I tried to put it out of my mind and hoped it would soon pass.

At the Mission guest house in Phnom Penh, I took a shower, expecting the cool water to alleviate the pain. It only intensified. I felt as though my blood was about to burst through the top of my head. It was evident that this was much more than just heat stroke.

I staggered out of the bathroom and fell into bed. That is where Miriam and Don found me when they arrived from Saigon.

How miserable I felt! I was drained of all strength and I couldn't eat or sleep as the pain worked its way out to the extremities of my body. Someone phoned a French doctor, who without seeing me, diagnosed my illness as malaria. He promised to come by and give me an injection. He never showed up.

Convinced in my heart that I would certainly die if the Lord did not heal me, I asked the missionaries to anoint and pray for me. After prayer, I felt encouraged that I might live, but I still suffered with intense pain. Another night of agony ensued.

About five o'clock the next morning a most wonderful thing happened. The Lord touched me! The sensation at the base of my spine was like holding a water bottle upside down and pulling the cork. The pain drained as if in one big gush from my head, my hands and my feet. I got out of bed praising the Lord. Free from the pain, I ate my first meal in three days.

Within a few weeks of my miracle the Japanese army made a bloodless invasion into Indochina. Not a shot was fired. The French regime became a puppet government.

Now it seemed that we were constantly being forced, always under severe time constraints, to make momentous decisions. With our second child about to be born, we had to decide whether to stay in Cambodia or go to the Philippines where the American flag still flew and the hospitals were well staffed. Inasmuch as the Japanese had already taken over all of Indochina, it seemed wise to head for the Philippines, a sure and safe haven. Little did we know what was soon to happen.

I gradually regained some strength and decided to send Miriam and Don ahead to Manila with other missionaries who were en route to the States for furlough. Marguerite Sechrist also went to Manila to await the birth of her second child. Harold and I stayed behind.

Shortly after the women left, Harold took ill and it was decided that he should leave immediately for Saigon for treatment. With our wives already in the Philippines and because of our physical condition, I got permission to meet Harold in Saigon and together we headed for Manila.

Hot, humid Manila. Miriam had a recurrence of dengue fever, so we, along with the Sechrists, moved up to the cool, mountain air of Baguio, a veritable tropical paradise compared to Manila. We rented a small vacation house belonging to the Presbyterians and later a larger place owned by a Filipino doctor. The Sechrists, however, became concerned about the possibility of war breaking out in the Philippines and they decided to return to Manila.

In Baguio, we met Dr. R.A. Jaffray, the great missionary pioneer of Asia who was on a short furlough before going back to Indonesia. It was a brief but blessed time of fellowship. He felt war was imminent in the Far East and, not wanting to get caught in the Philippines, he left for Indonesia on a ship which was probably the last one out of Manila harbor.

On December 8, 1941, we were awakened by frightening news—the Japanese had bombed Pearl

Harbor. On that same day, only hours later, Japanese bombers began pummelling beautiful Baguio and the military bases in the Philippines. The war was on in earnest.

The Philippine Air Force was, for the most part, destroyed on the ground the first day of the attack. That meant that Japanese planes now controlled the air. Large Japanese troop contingents landed on the shores below Baugio. The superior Japanese forces soon broke through the resistance of the Americans and Filipinos. The islands were literally being overrun.

To see the collapse of the Filipino social order was an emotional experience beyond description. All U.S. citizens were advised by Colonel Horan to pack an emergency bag and be ready for any eventuality. Not only did we do as suggested, but we scurried from store to store stocking up on any food we could get our hands on—powdered milk for Don and the new baby; flour, soap, toilet paper, toothpaste and canned goods of all kinds. Hundreds of others were doing the same thing. There was virtual pandemonium in the streets and markets. Fear and panic were evident on everyone's face. Planes roared overhead daily. We ran for shelter. It was a desperate situation.

Miriam and I discussed our future. More decisions had to be made. We agreed that Don and I would walk Miriam to Notre Dame Hospital each evening before the curfew at dark. If there was no bombing, she would walk home the next morning providing the baby hadn't arrived. This became our daily ritual for the next few days.

On Wednesday evening, December 24th, Miriam suggested we leave Don with friends and I stay at the hospital with her overnight. It turned out to be a wise decision, for Janice Allaine Taylor arrived early Christmas morning, 1941.

When I visited Miriam the next morning, Friday, we decided that Don and I should move in with some Baptist friends at Doane Rest, a sizable missionary compound next door to a Japanese school. I borrowed a car and transported our belongings including the boxes of food that had cost us $400, our last funds on hand. By the time I had finished moving, the Japanese military was cruising around the city and although I had planned to return to the hospital, it seemed impractical and perhaps even dangerous to try to venture out on the streets again.

By early evening that same day we began to hear the Japanese next door celebrating their victory with a big bonfire and shouting "Banzai (victory)." Sleep was impossible.

Uncertainty, like a dark cloud, hung over us. We were facing an unknown future. Don and I were holed up at the missionary compound. Miriam and Janice, we hoped, were still in the hospital. We could not reach them nor could we find out how they were faring. I prayed. And waited.

At midnight, there was a loud pounding on the front door accompanied by shouts in a foreign language that needed no interpretation. I was elected as a committee of one to go down and let the visitors in.

As I swung the big wooden door open, five rifles

were thrust in my face. The Japanese ordered me upstairs. With guns at the back of my head, I climbed the stairs to get Don and to pack some belongings. As I entered our bedroom, a horrific explosion sounded out in the hall. A nervous gunman had accidently pulled the trigger.

We were ordered out to the front yard. The other missionaries on the compound had already been rounded up and were being pushed into a waiting car. By the time Don and I reached the car there was hardly room for us, let alone our bags. With the promise, "We take bag tomorrow," a soldier pushed us in on top of the others and hauled us away. Our bags never followed. Don and I were left with no food and only the clothes on our backs.

We soon found ourselves at Brent School where we were herded into a two-story building along with several hundred other Americans. During the tense, sleepless nights before our capture Don and I had not been able to eat. Now, in this incredible situation, we were smitten with violent hunger. But we had nothing to eat. Those more fortunate sat eating the food they had brought along.

Hours passed. Where were Miriam and baby Janice? Were they still at the hospital? I had seen the baby only three times. Was she all right? Was Miriam all right? What was she told when I didn't appear yesterday? When would we be reunited? Such questions swirled in my mind and ripped at my soul.

All day Sunday we waited for food while the Japanese brought in more and more prisoners. Finally, Monday noon, we were served some watered-down stew made from meat confiscated from the butcher shop of an Australian fellow prisoner. We had been in Brent School three days.

Later that day we were all ordered out of Brent School, taking with us only what we could carry for the march to Camp John Hay. Don and I had nothing to carry, so we helped others with their loads. The streets were lined with Filipinos staring at the dejected Americans in their hour of defeat.

At Camp John Hay we were put into one single barracks—500 of us! There was room only for us to lie down on the floor, row upon row, men, women and children. The barracks were continually patrolled by Japanese guards with fixed bayonets.

More than a week passed and still no word about Miriam. The American doctors had been captured with us, so obviously this left only Filipino nurses in charge at the hospital.

That first week in Camp John Hay many children came down with dysentery because of the unsanitary conditions—500 people using toilets that were clogged and overflowing. More and more cases broke out every day. Screaming in pain, the sickest children were taken to Notre Dame Hospital. The Japanese allowed one of our American doctors to accompany them.

One day, when Dr. Allen returned from one of these trips to the hospital, she called me aside.

"Harry, your wife is dying," she said. "Hemorrhaging badly. She's still in Notre Dame Hospital."

I was devastated. The last horror-filled week had seemed like an eternity. Now, the question that dominated every waking moment was, "Would I ever see my wife and daughter again?"

"Let's go together to the Japanese commandant," Dr. Allen suggested. "Maybe he will let you go and see her."

The commandant's answer was an indignant, "No."

I pleaded, "But she is dying!"

"So what? Many people are dying," he snarled.

We were ordered back to the barracks.

Part II

The Philippines:
Behind Barbed Wire

*We have escaped like a bird
out of the fowler's snare; . . .
Our help is in the name of the LORD,
the Maker of heaven and earth.
(Psalm 124:7a, 8)*

6

Camp John Hay

(Miriam)

The war had been going on since December 8th, now three weeks. There had been no way of escape. We were caught! I was in Notre Dame Hospital and Janice was two days old. I felt weak. I cried. I tried to pray. I committed the whole situation into the hands of the Lord. I meditated on my life-verse: "As for God, his way is perfect; the word of the LORD is flawless. He is a shield for all who take refuge in him" (Psalm 18:30).

My present circumstances certainly didn't look very perfect. And yet I knew this verse was true. It had to be true. God said it!

Fortunately I had my Bible with me in the hospital. I didn't have much else. Inside the cover I found a tract that a friend had sent me before we left Cambodia.

At that time, I hadn't really been able to see how it would ever apply to me. But now, in unpredicted, undesirable circumstances, there was new meaning: "The Lord will keep thee in all thy ways." The Lord would keep me "sweet," it said, in a "sour" place, "cool" in a "hot" place, "quiet" in a "noisy" place and "clean" in a "dirty" place. The tract went on to say that my experiences would result in personal spiritual enrichment and that God's own hand would determine the timing and the length of the trial.

As I reread the tract in the hospital room I began to see God's hand in the events that had brought us here. We had come to the Philippines to have our baby. It had seemed to be the right decision. We dared not doubt. We knew the Lord would continue to lead us.

Then came the bombing of the Philippines by the Japanese and the sudden invasion. Those roaring planes. The explosions that followed. There were no air-raid shelters. No one knew where to run for protection.

At night, there were no street lights. All windows were covered with dark paper. How could we explain our present predicament to four-year-old Don?

Chills often ran up and down my spine. I had a sick feeling in the pit of my stomach and tightness in my chest most of the time. When would I have the baby? Where would I have the baby? Would I be able to get to the hospital at the right time, if at all? Would I be safe even there?

Then we heard that the Japanese had landed at Lingayen Gulf, just 18 miles down the mountain from Baguio. Harry and I discussed what we should do. We prayed and we waited.

I already had my small bag packed to go to the hospital—one outfit for me, one for the baby.

Should I take more? Just in case? I began to sort through our things. What should I throw away? What should I set aside? I threw all but one of my maternity dresses in the corner of the room. I never wanted to see them again. I kept out the best one to wear to the hospital.

It was the night before Christmas. I suggested to Harry that we ask our missionary friends across the street to keep Don for the night so that Harry could stay with me at the hospital.

Christmas morning 1941, at 7:30, Janice Allaine Taylor was born—the most precious Christmas present I have ever received. At the time of the delivery I was blissfully unaware that my doctor was drunk, and I was, therefore, unprepared for the consequences.

Harry spent part of Christmas day with Don. The rest of the day he stayed with me at the hospital. We talked about our little family. We praised God for all His blessings. We tried to put aside the ominous happenings around us, but it was impossible.

The second day we discussed what to do with our belongings. By now, rumors were running wild. Would Baguio be taken over by the Japanese invading forces or would they head toward Manila first? We decided that it might be a good idea for Harry and Don to move into Doane Rest with friends. Once again we were finding it difficult to make decisions under these circumstances for any decision might be the wrong one. No one, including us, knew what to do. But it did help to at least have a plan.

On December 28th Harry did not show up at the

hospital. I was worried. Rumors had it that the Japanese were coming up the mountain and would be in town very soon.

When a Filipino nurse came into my room, I mentioned that my husband had not come to see me.

"He won't be coming either," she said.

Harry wouldn't be coming? Why not? Had something happened to him? And what about little Don? I could only guess what she was trying to tell me.

After a moment's pause, she continued.

"Last night the Japanese came into town and rounded up all the American and British citizens and put them in Brent School. That is all I know at this point." With that, she left the room.

I tried to imagine what was going on outside the hospital walls. The bombings had stopped. That much I knew. Somehow the quietness didn't seem quite so dangerous. But what about Harry and Don? Were they really safe or were they in danger?

As these thoughts churned in my head, the nurse returned and began recounting a conversation she had just had with a Japanese officer.

"He told me that all of the Americans and British will soon be eating dirt," she confided.

Chills once more ran up and down my spine. The only thing that came to my mind was, *What about my baby?*

I did not feel well. I was flushed and feverish. I tried to walk around the room, but felt faint and collapsed onto the bed. The hospital doctor had been taken away with the rest of the Americans. I needed someone to help me.

My stomach began to swell and I started to

hemorrhage. *Am I going to die?* I wondered. *Who will take care of Janice?*

I prayed, "Oh, Lord, it doesn't matter about our belongings. Just please take us through this ordeal and some day get all four of us back to the States."

Turning my head toward the door I noticed a stranger. Hesitantly she moved closer to my bed.

"I was walking down the street in front of the hospital," she said, "and God told me that someone needed me here. Because I am Danish they didn't take me with the rest to Brent School. I'm a registered nurse."

She looked at me and at my blood-soaked bed and immediately realized my condition. Throwing off her sweater, she began to massage my stomach unmercifully. Even though the pain was excruciating, she persisted with the treatment until the remaining portion of the afterbirth had been dislodged. She gave me some medication and tried to make me as comfortable as possible. Then she said goodbye. I never saw her again.

Later, as the Danish nurse had instructed, I was taken into the operating room for follow-up procedures. Improvement was slow. I couldn't sit up or feed myself, but each day I felt a little stronger.

To add to my troubles, since the beginning of the month American and British children from Camp John Hay had been arriving at the hospital with dysentery. Some were very sick and screaming with pain.

I kept asking the nurses, "Is Don Taylor, my son, among the children?"

Thankfully, the answer was always "no."

The first time I tried to lower my feet to the floor, a Japanese guard poked his head into my room.

"Tomorrow camp!" he announced sharply.

I didn't answer, but I thought, *I can't even walk, yet. How am I going to go to the camp?*

January 16, 1942

Yesterday a nurse wheeled me out of the hospital to the camp vegetable truck and helped me up into the front seat beside the driver. My three-week-old baby was placed on my lap and off we went. What an experience! The driver couldn't speak any English and I didn't know Japanese. He had come to town to get food for the 500 internees and was taking me back with him.

We drove a few miles. Then he stopped the truck in a wooded area and left me alone. I couldn't see where he went.

After a few minutes, which seemed like hours, he reappeared, his arms filled with flowers. He put the bouquet on my lap as much as to say, "I am sorry." Perhaps he had a wife and children back in Japan. I didn't know.

As we approached the camp, I wondered if I would be permitted to see Harry and Don. The weeks we had been separated seemed like a year.

Sure enough! Harry and Don were at the gate to greet us. What a reunion! They helped me get to an already crowded storeroom with only one little window at the far end. My floor mat and the basket for Janice were squeezed into a small space not occupied by 12 other mothers and their babies. The congestion and the noise grated on my nerves.

Once Janice and I were safely deposited, Harry and Don were ushered back to the men's barracks next door. There was so much I wanted to tell Harry and so many questions I wanted to ask him. Would they ever let us spend some time together to talk about all that had happened during our month of separation?

January 26, 1942

The Japanese commandant announced several days ago that interrogations were to begin. It is apparent that the only group in our camp on the list to be interrogated are missionaries. Most of those called are recent arrivals from China, forced to withdraw because of the Japanese invasion there. It is obvious missionaries are prime suspects of the Japanese. They can't imagine anyone being anything but spies in a foreign country.

Japanese army trucks drove into our camp and took a group of missionaries downtown to intelligence headquarters for interrogation. My heart sank as I saw Harry shoved into the waiting truck. Along with the other wives, I was sick all day wondering if our men would return. Yesterday three did not return. Why? No one seems to know.

January 29, 1942

All missionaries were told to assemble on the tennis court. We stood around discussing the possible motive for this summons. Then the camp commandant announced that tomorrow, at exactly two o'clock, we missionaries are to be ready to leave camp. We can't believe our ears. Are we to be set free so soon?

7

Camp Holmes

(Miriam)

January 30, 1942

It's true! Today, first thing in the morning, carrying our few possessions, we were put onto trucks and transported into town. A number of us were taken to Doane Rest. Our Japanese guards, finding that Doane Rest was already occupied by some Japanese, ordered us to spend the night in the Japanese school next door. We couldn't help but wonder about the possessions we had recently abandoned there and especially about the suitcase Harry had packed but was never delivered. Fortunately, some other internees had extra and were willing to share with us.

It is now long after dark. We are so weary and so hungry. Janice is on the floor beside me. A little while ago a Japanese lady came into the room and noticed the rolled up blanket on the floor. When she saw that the blanket held a tiny baby girl, she dropped to her knees and stared. After several moments, she disappeared upstairs.

Other members of the Japanese family came into the room with stacks of pancakes and syrup. Could they have been made from our very own pancake mix we had left in the house next door? In any case, we ate until our stomachs were full—for the first time since the last of December, four weeks ago.

After we finished eating, the lady, in full Japanese attire, returned carrying a gift in both outstretched hands as is their custom. She went over to the little bundle on the floor, made several deep bows, then, down on her knees, she laid the attractively wrapped package at Janice's feet. After a few minutes, she stood up and once again disappeared. I opened the gift. It was a beautiful child's kimono.

January 31, 1942

We slept fitfully last night due to the hard floor and the uncertainty as to what the future might hold. Now that we are released from internment camp and since we have no money, possessions or place to live, the situation looks rather bleak.

Our uncertainty was short-lived, for at dawn a Japanese official appeared to tell us that there had been a mistake in interpreting the army telegram from Manila. It had read, "Release Baguio missionaries." We were informed that the supposed intention of the telegram was to release only those actually doing missionary work in Baguio City.

February 3, 1942

Only 24 hours of freedom. Now we are back in Camp John Hay.

Our unexpected return presented a real problem. During our short absence, the other internees took over our sleeping spots on the floor. Sleeping space had to be reassigned to accommodate the large group of returned missionaries. It was an unpleasant experience both for those who had to give up some inches of space on the floor and for us, too. We felt rather unwelcome.

February 16, 1942

We have been given numbers to wear. Men, women and children.

February 18, 1942

Husbands and wives are allowed to meet on Sunday afternoon for half an hour on the tennis courts. Today Harry told me about his interrogation.

He was driven into Baguio and taken to the military police headquarters located in a downtown hotel. Watching others being unmercifully kicked reinforced the seriousness of the situation.

The men were shut up in a waiting room with nothing to hold their attention but fear of the impending interrogation. Harry's name was called and he was ushered into one of the interrogation rooms and told to sit down at a desk. Left alone for a short time, his eyes were drawn to the instruments of torture hanging on the walls. On the desk was a paper with a list of names. Harry saw his name with several red check marks after it. Not very reassuring!

Then, in marched a young man who served as a Japanese interpreter. He ordered Harry to stand up as a Japanese officer with thick glasses stomped in. The officer flopped into a chair on the other side of the desk and ordered Harry to sit down.

Checking over the list of prisoners, the officer

confirmed Harry's name through the interpreter. To unnerve Harry, the officer would begin his questioning in a low tone and end the sentence in a high, screaming voice. Frightening! The Japanese interpreter attempted to duplicate both the message and the sentiment!

They correctly identified Harry as a recent arrival in the Philippines, but had his previous address as Shanghai, China. This rang a bell in Harry's mind. He recalled hearing of a radio news reporter in Shanghai who was famous for his anti-Japanese broadcasts castigating Japan for its ruthless invasion of China. The broadcaster's name was Harry Taylor! Obviously the Japanese army couldn't wait to get their hands on Harry Taylor. That explained the red check marks.

When they found that Harry had come from Cambodia and had never been to Shanghai, they were disarmed. After a few moments of verbal fumbling, they sent him back unscathed to the waiting room.

It was long after dark when the men returned to camp. Some of them had been beaten and others were given the water treatment (water poured into the mouth without letup, giving the sensation of being drowned). They were then brought back to consciousness for further questioning and hopefully a confession.

Except for the Sunday rendezvous on the tennis courts, husbands and wives cannot meet or speak to each other even though our barracks are next to each other. Fortunately, I get a glimpse of Harry once a day when the men pass our barracks for morning roll call. At least I know he is still okay.

Children are permitted to come and go from one barracks to the other, so Don, now almost five, carries messages back and forth. This helps our morale.

Of the 500 people in our camp, about 150 are missionaries. One third are miners who worked in the nearby gold mines and the remainder are professional (quite a few doctors) and business people. There are about 50 children.

April 10, 1942

A notice is posted by the Japanese every time American forces are defeated. Today we read, "Bataan fell April 9, 1942."

April 14, 1942

A truck drove in today with two of the three missionaries who had been detained since January. The third missionary, Rufus Gray, a Baptist, was not with them. Will he ever return?

April 20, 1942

It has been rumored that we will be moved to Camp Holmes, another military camp on the other side of Baguio. The reason for the move? They say there will be more space.

By now we are becoming accustomed to camp life. We have what we call "close association"—500 people in a crowded space learning to adjust to each other. Considering the fact that we don't have very much privacy, we do fairly well. The most difficult aspect is uncertainty of the future. How long must we live behind barbed wire?

April 23, 1942

Trucks came thick and fast. It took only five hours to move all the personnel and possessions to our new location at Camp Holmes, about 12 kilometers from Baguio. We were taken through the city of Baguio past Trinidad Valley, out the Bontoc road. Then we turned to the right into Camp Holmes, a former Filipino constabulary which had been built on the side of the mountain. Passing the guard house, we moved across the expansive parade grounds to the three barracks which are proving to be more spacious than those at Camp John Hay.

Down the hill, set apart from the army barracks, are two buildings. The camp committee decided to use one for a hospital and the other for mothers with small children—about 16 of us. Again, I am separated from Harry and little Donald. The whole camp is surrounded by barbed wire fencing and secured by armed Japanese guards.

April 28, 1942

Harry has noticed increasing atrophy in his right leg. A Jewish doctor diagnosed it as being the result of polio. Now we know what that awful sickness in Phnom Penh was.

May 15, 1942

I'm still not strong at all. I can hardly swallow my allotted portions of food. Two young women, Judy Skogerbo and Esther Olson, Lutheran missionaries, noticed my plight and have given me their precious bottle of Lextron vitamin/iron pills. What a blessing! They are giving me strength.

Judy and Esther were transferred from China just before the war started. If I ever have another daughter I'll name her Judith Esther.

May 30, 1942

Our diet is still limited. The Japanese do not have as much to be concerned about since the American forces have retreated to Australia. So the rules are somewhat relaxed. Once in a while I can talk to Harry in chow line and in the dining room.

We are permitted to buy at Franklin Mount's store—if we have any money. Being penniless ourselves, we have been able to borrow from those who have. The money is to be paid back after the war.

The camp buyer was willing to take my diamond ring into town and sell it for cash. We bought peanuts with the money. We grind them into peanut-butter with the army kitchen grinder. We also bought corn to grind into cornmeal. We hope to get some native sugar soon. This will help supplement our short rations.

We don't know how long these privileges will last. It seems that some of the Japanese commandants want to help us, but others do all they can to make life as difficult as possible.

Committees run the activities of our small village. Each internee is expected to work a certain number of hours each day. Harry has been assigned to be the camp barber.

What qualifies him? I wonder. The day he was taken from Doane Rest, with only the clothes on his back, he slipped his barber's comb, scissors and clippers into his pocket because Don needed a haircut. Later in camp when Harry began shearing Don, he looked up to see a line of men and boys waiting their turn. Harry is also on the burial committee and we have both been assigned to teach French to some high school students.

July 6, 1942

Somehow news from the outside is getting into camp. We're hearing more and more details of what's become known as "The Bataan Death March."

Six days after surrender, thousands of Filipino and American soldiers were forced to march in columns of four for 60 miles under the searing tropical sun. Literally dying of thirst and hunger, they watched their guards throw food away. Anyone caught with Japanese money or what may have been stolen from enemy dead were beaten to death.

Behind the main lines, mop-up squads killed those who fell because they were sick, exhausted or abused. Thousands of casualties. Few escaped.

July 20, 1942

Dr. Doug Tyson has taken special interest in Harry's leg. He has been massaging it. In spite of some improvement, Harry still limps noticeably.

December 23, 1942

Today is my birthday. I'm 28. It seems like I should be 40 by now. Harry made me two dozen clothes pins from split bamboo. A note enclosed with the gift said, "This coupon is good for two weeks free wash!" Don's contribution is to come down and get our dirty clothes and take them up to

Harry to wash, then return them to me when they're dry.

In two days Janice will have her first birthday. She's spent her first year behind barbed wire. Her grandparents don't even know about her. We haven't been able to send any word yet. No letters have reached us either. Do our families know we're still alive?

January 3, 1943

Because we are so many missionaries in camp the commandant has given us permission to have one Sunday service a month. Each denominational group will take its turn leading these services. Also, there are several Bible studies taught by volunteers. Restrictions for worship are gradually being relaxed.

January 8, 1943

Among the women the major conversation is about food. Some even spend time copying recipes from each other. Why the intense interest in food? We are hungry most of the time. Meals are served only twice a day from the communal dining room. We have to make our own arrangements for a noon snack. The peanuts and corn we bought are almost gone.

January 11, 1943

Our Camp Holmes Civilian Internment Camp No. 3 Committee wrote a letter to the Highest Commander of the Philippine Islands urgently appealing for more food. Anemia, beri-beri and other illnesses resulting from malnutrition are increasing at an alarming rate. The doctors predict irreparable damage to our health—even death for some—if immediate steps are not taken.

June 16, 1943

The *Camp Daily News* posted on the bulletin board reads: "Life continues. It's eventless, meatless, sugarless, flourless, matchless, margarineless, comfortless, meaningless. Yet we go on."

December 20, 1943

Soon it will be our second Christmas as POWs. Harry couldn't wait to give me my birthday present—a pin depicting a typical Baguio scene with a mountain in the background, a thatch-roofed house, buffalo and rice field, all etched with a nail into a piece of coconut shell. It is wired to a one-inch by two-inch piece of cow bone which forms a frame. A safety pin is reshaped and wired to the back for a clasp. What a work of art!

Our new army commandant is Mr. Tomibe. He is stern, demands respect, but has a keen sense of justice and compassion. He shows concern and tries to help us. He has allowed more self-rule in the camp. He even issues passes to go to the hill above the camp for picnics! Roll calls are often taken in the barracks by monitors instead of guards. He is also open to suggestions for making life more bearable.

December 24, 1943

What excitement! Today seven large trucks rolled into camp with Red Cross food kits. Last year's shipment never reached us! It must have been distributed in Manila for lack of transportation the 150 miles to Baguio. Or maybe it was confiscated.

The trucks brought 520 boxes—one for each person. We each received a 47-pound box of food— cheese, milk powder, chocolate bars, butter in tins and canned meat. There were also some luxuries— facial tissues, handkerchiefs, laundry and face soap. Even shoe polish, but most of us don't have shoes. We wear wooden clogs made for us in the camp. Also, we were each given a bath towel, a sheet, a comb, a pencil and some clothing—underwear, a nightgown and a playsuit for each of the women. What a delight!

Dr. and Mrs. Marshall Wells and their two boys, Presbyterian medical missionaries, and our family have decided to ration our boxes of food and share with each other. Whenever we open a can of food, we divide it into eight portions. Hopefully this will make our supply last twice as long.

March 17, 1944

A Family Unit Project was proposed in the camp executive committee meeting today. This will allow families to live together cubicle style. There is to be a sign-up sheet.

April 5, 1944

A devastating development! At evening roll call we heard that two prisoners escaped—Herbert Swick and Richard Green. Both had been issued a pass for the hill today. Mr. Tomibe is very upset. He trusted us. He tried to make life more bearable for us. He says we have betrayed and embarrassed him. He holds us accountable.

April 7, 1944

At intervals different internees are taken away and questioned, especially close friends of the escapees. Bill Moule returned to camp, but Gene Kneebone and Jim Halsema were kept. The Japanese tried to get information from them by hanging them by their thumbs. Ropes on pulleys hoisted them up till their toes barely touched the floor. This caused excruciating pain. Bill said he was hung this way four times in four hours, 20 minutes at a time. The men were also severely beaten.

April 16, 1944

A petition against the cubicle plan for families was circulated. Many are adamantly opposed. I can't understand why only 50 of the 97 married couples have signed up.

April 19, 1944

Bits and pieces of the puzzle have come together about the two who escaped. Supposedly the escapees left to join the American and Filipino guerrilla forces in the mountains. They left after dark April 4th. Because they had passes to go up the mountain for a picnic the morning of the 5th, they were not missed until that evening. They had a 24-hour head start.

We have suffered for their action. Stringent camp rules have been reinstituted. Mr. Tomibe himself is in charge of roll call, no longer held in the barracks, but on the parade ground twice a day. An eight-foot bamboo fence has been built outside the barbed wire fence. No more passes for picnics. Additional guards have been assigned to our camp. We fear Mr. Tomibe will be held responsible and replaced.

April 28, 1944

The cubicle plan went into effect today. This entailed moving again and reassigning spaces. What an enormous job!

The "baby house" where Janice and I have lived will be rearranged to accommodate eight families with 13 children instead of the 16 mothers and babies of the past. Mothers with older children are to move topside to the barracks up the hill.

We plan to place our sleeping mats on boards and hang them from the rafters. This will give us space underneath for a makeshift table and stools. We will need a ladder to get up to the sleeping loft.

I can't imagine being together as a family and having so much space to ourselves. Of course, there will be three other families in the same room. The elevated platforms will hopefully help to protect us from nibbling rats.

May 15, 1944

The camp livestock includes a cow and a few goats, good sources of milk. But the inevitable has happened—the cow and the goats have gone dry. One of my duties for the camp is to pasteurize the milk for the smaller children. What are we going to do? In the past, when beans were available, we ground them to augment the milk supply. (During our internment so far, the children's milk supply has come from at least five different sources—the mothers, cows, water buffaloes, goats and several kinds of beans.)

May 20, 1944

At our prayer meeting last night we asked God to send us milk. Early this morning, five cows were found standing at the camp gate. The Japanese guards were persuaded by the camp leaders to open the gates and let them in. No one knows where they came from. Perhaps they were searching for salt. Some say, "It just happened," but we believe God sent them to us in answer to prayer. Several are milk cows. The rest we hopefully will be allowed to keep for meat.

September 15, 1944

Mr. Tomibe gave a farewell speech at roll call. He told us that he has been transferred to Manila. We will all miss him.

November 15, 1944

Suddenly, planes buzzed our camp. Instead of a big red sun on the wings and fuselage, they had big white stars. U.S. Navy planes! Our hopes soared. We are beginning to look forward to liberation. We think of General MacArthur's promise three years ago, "I shall return." What excitement! But we dare not show our joy because of threatened abuse.

November 27, 1944

It's almost our third Christmas in prison. Still no word from our families. We sent one 25-word Red Cross message on a three-by-five card to Harry's folks. I wonder if they ever received it.

December 26, 1944

We have just been told we will be moved again—

this time to Manila. Hot, humid Manila. Sixty percent of us will go on Thursday, the 28th, and the
rest on Friday, the 29th. Many are complaining.
No one is pleased with this order. Baguio has always been famous as a mountain resort because of
its altitude, scenery and pleasant climate.

We have been ordered to take only limited baggage. In our case, that won't be a hardship—we
have very little to worry about.

We hear via the grapevine that the Americans
have already landed on the island of Leyte. Is it
possible that we might get caught in some fighting
on the way to Manila? We don't know what to expect.

8

Bilibid Prison

(Miriam)

December 28, 1944

Just 36 hours after the relocation announcement, the move became a reality. Trucks were commandeered and four soldiers guarded each vehicle as we traveled down the mountain perched on top of boxes and baggage in the back of the truck. There was no railing to keep us from falling overboard and no shelter from sun or rain.

Harry and I sat back to back facing the opposite sides of the truck with the children between us. Our feet were braced against the top of the sideboards for support. We had to be very watchful as the heavily loaded trucks occasionally passed under overhanging rocks. One man was decapitated on the trip.

The truck stopped at Binalonan in the lowlands at the junction of the road to Manila. We were ordered to get off and unload the baggage. The Army needed the trucks, they said.

While we waited for our next instructions we ate

the lunch we had brought with us—meat from some of the cows the Lord had sent to our camp. Then we started to rearrange our few possessions. We placed them in a sheet to suspend from a bamboo pole we found by the side of the road. We also prepared a small bundle for Don to carry. He is now almost eight. Janice, only three, wanted to carry the doll someone had given her.

We were finally told we would have to walk to Manila as no trucks had been located to transport us the rest of the way. Actually, it would have been impossible to walk to Manila but we had no choice but to start out. Harry and I shouldered the pole with all of our earthly possessions dangling between us. Don had his pack and Janice her doll. She soon became so weary that, in tears, she threw it down at the side of the road. Harry has a very troublesome toothache.

Mercifully, it began to rain and the Japanese ordered us all to take shelter in the bamboo nipa huts along the side of the road. One of the Taiwanese guards slipped us some dried shrimp from his lunch.

Long after dark the rain stopped and Japanese trucks came to take us the rest of the way. The continuous changing of instructions and directions gives us a constant sense of uncertainty and insecurity. About midnight we were finally pushed up on top of all the baggage in the overloaded truck. On the way to Manila, we passed literally thousands of Japanese soldiers walking in the opposite direction, heading to the north end of the island. Could they be marching to meet McArthur's forces?

We traveled all night. The air was hot and laden

with humidity. The stretch on the lowlands was long. Those who were sick with diarrhea kept calling out in pain for the truck to stop, but it didn't. Finally, about sunrise, we arrived at the old Bilibid Prison. The massive gates swung open to let us in, then closed behind us as though swallowing us whole.

We stood for some time in front of the main building awaiting roll call. Some fainted from the combination of heat and fatigue.

December 30, 1944

The filth in this prison is unbelievable! How can it be described? Piles of contaminated mattresses filled with ticks and bedbugs and stained from diarrhea are piled in the yard. They cannot be used. The scout team of internees who preceded us have done their best to prepare the place, but what a task!

Along the prison walls rows of wooden crosses mark the graves of American soldiers who died in the prison. Their dog tags are draped over the crosses. What horrors lay behind the scene before us?

And the rats! They scurry around and over the piles of garbage and filthy mattresses.

The compound is about 200 feet wide and 600 feet long, with 16-foot high walls surrounding it. The building is just a two-story shell with corrugated iron sheets at the large open windows. As for toilets, they are open and outside in full view. The internee crew is trying to make them a little more private. Bluebottle flies are everywhere! How can we possibly escape disease?

Five hundred people have to wash at several tin sinks along the wall. There are also roofless showers along the yard wall, the only bathing facilities.

January 2, 1945

There is another section of the prison separated from us by a high wall. Survivors of the Bataan Death March are held there. We can't see them, but we have heard nails being pounded. Coffins, they say.

Before we arrived, about 1,600 able-bodied survivors were put on a ship headed for Japan. Some say they will be sent to Manchuria.

January 5, 1945

Instructions of the commandant (interpretation by Mr. S. Yamoto): "It has suddenly occurred that we transferred you to Manila by the order of the Japanese military authorities. I think you were vexed much by so sudden a removal. This building you are to live in is in construction, without complete equipment, and very probably caused you dissatisfactions and inconvenience. I am very sorry on that point. Of course, I am intent on supplying you with various conveniences, but to my regret, owing to the shortage of materials in Manila, everything cannot be done as I wish to do. As to food, it is also my regret to say I cannot supply as much as I wish. At present every belligerent country is suffering from shortage of food and material. And I hear that even your native country is also among the rest. Not only you alone but also I and my subordinates are all living in this place and are taking the same food as you. Now, I am obliged to tell you to be patient. Some day peace will come to all of us. Observe the orders of the Japanese Army and taking good care of yourselves, wait for the coming of peace in quiet perseverance." Major Ebiko, The Commandant of the Japanese Army, Internment Camp No. 3.

January 6, 1945

A notice was posted today insisting we strictly obey the air raid protection rules. Many pieces of shrapnel have fallen within the camp and there are no hospital facilities for removing shrapnel splinters and bomb fragments.

January 7, 1945

Another notice was placed on the wall regarding our water situation. Should a bomb destroy the water main to the north of us, we would be in serious trouble. We are urged to keep every available container filled with water at all times. There are no reserve water tanks.

January 8, 1945

Lt. Oura visited our camp. He came on an inspection tour and we were told he was most displeased. He ordered that all north windows in the main building must be closed and remain closed; the ends of the porches must be boarded up with galvanized tin. Despite the protests of our executive committee that closing the windows would make it too hot and stuffy with no breeze or light, he said it must be done.

On his way past the wall in the front of the hospital, Lt. Oura cut some clothes lines full of clothes simply because they were in his way. Before leaving, Lt. Oura expressed great displeasure over the lack of response and bowing to him. He declared that in the future, if anyone did not bow to him, he will knock that person across the head or put him in jail.

January 10, 1945

Our camp executive committee reported that the Japanese plan for Manila to be declared a protected city rather than an open city. This change will probably come soon.

January 18, 1945

Fortunately, we brought our mats and mosquito nets with us from Baguio. They not only keep us from being bitten by the mosquitoes but also from being nipped by the roving rats at night. It is scary. We also use our nets for a little privacy in the overcrowded quarters housing men, women and children. We undress after dark and dress before daylight under our nets.

The heat of Manila is stifling both day and night. We aren't used to hot, humid weather.

Although we're not pleased to be in Manila, the move was indeed providential. We have heard that Camp Holmes has been completely destroyed by U.S. Air Force bombings!

January 20, 1945

We found out that some of our fellow internees have been secretly listening to a radio built back in Camp Holmes from old telephone parts. By tuning into American forces radio they learned that our troops have indeed landed at Lingayen Gulf, about 125 miles north of Manila.

Food is very scarce. We are so glad we decided to ration our Red Cross packages with the Wells. We have some left, but don't know how long it will be before we are liberated, so we must still be cautious.

Harry's toothache is getting more uncomfortable. No relief. We have eight missionary doctors, but no medicine.

Today I found Don rummaging in a Japanese garbage can. I already knew he was hungry, but it saddened me to see him that hungry.

We are fed only twice a day and not much at that. For breakfast: cornmeal mush with cassava root, soft rice with cassava root, soybeans, some sort of tea. For lunch: nothing. For dinner: boiled rice, talinum greens grown in Bilibid Prison, and miso (fermented soy bean).

While still in Baguio I had occasionally removed a tablespoon of rice from each bowl. Then I dried the cooked rice in a wood stove oven until it was very hard. Storing it in a discarded, airtight milk can, I hid it for more difficult days ahead. Now I dish out some of this rice, pour boiling water over it and serve it to the children at midday when no meal is served.

January 25, 1945

We are all very thin and many of us have swollen joints—a sign of beri-beri. We feel weak from the slightest exertion. Food is at a premium. We don't know how long we will be able to endure the present situation. Dysentery and dengue fever are spreading through the camp. A temporary hospital has been set up here in Bilibid but is fast filling to capacity. A patient, if only the slightest bit improved, has to move out to make room for another who is in greater need of care.

The war in the city rages on. Explosions come ever closer to us. We have gotten so experienced that we can judge the battle front's distance from us by counting the seconds between seeing the light and hearing the explosion. We feel confident liberation is in sight!

February 1, 1945

We are told the 1st Cavalry broke down the closed gates of Santo Tomás University Internment Camp about five blocks from us. We could hear the explosions. About 60 Japanese soldiers are holding a number of internees hostage in one of the buildings. Surely we will be next!

February 3, 1945

In Santo Tomás, after two days of shooting, the Japanese soldiers surrendered. In order to save the hostages, the Americans promised to let the soldiers return to Japanese lines.

We hear the humming of tanks coming nearer and nearer. Some think these are Japanese tanks in retreat. Others say, "No! They have to be American tanks!"

Screaming artillery and small arms fire pull us back to reality. Then all bedlam breaks loose. As night falls, some of the Japanese guards come into our building and climb the stairs to the roof. We can't believe it. Their intent must be to shoot at American forces in the area. In the city fires break out in every direction. The night is almost as light as day.

All of a sudden we can hear English being spoken. The army and marines are just outside our walls. But the Japanese haven't left yet! Rumors are flying through the prison. Hopes are really high. Surely, we'll soon be free!

February 4, 1945

The Japanese soldiers are still on the roof this morning. The American forces are securing the area around the prison. They must know we are here.

Yamoto, our commandant, turns to those near him and says sadly, "Goodbye, I am going to meet my fate."

Tanks are advancing outside our walls. We feel like we are on the front lines of this war in Manila.

Mid-morning, the Japanese give our camp leader release papers. At noon we are called together and our release is official. A notice has been placed on the iron gate, "Lawfully released prisoners of war and internees are quartered here."

While we are still congregated, the Japanese soldiers come down from the roof. We make a path for them to pass through, never to see them again.

Tears stream down our faces.

9

Home at Last

(Miriam)

We spontaneously broke out singing "God Bless America." Then an American flag that some women had been secretly working on for weeks was brought out of hiding and hoisted up on a bamboo pole. Then we sang "The Star-Spangled Banner" and began to cheer.

As we were cheering, a huge explosion suddenly reverberated across the city and a 12-inch plate of steel came hurtling into our compound over the heads of the cheering internees. It struck the building in front of us. We thought the Japanese were punishing us for celebrating. Later we learned that, in retreat, the Japanese had blown up Jones Bridge about a mile away.

Fires burned all day throughout the city and spread toward our prison. Demolition dumps were blown up. The smoke almost obliterated the sun.

About 6 p.m., members of the 37th Division infantry entered the prison. They told us we would have to be moved out of the city. They feared the prison might be mined.

We could see the firey conflagration coming closer each moment. If it reached our gates we would be trapped with no way of escape. The U.S. Army decided to move us out immediately—500 internees along with the remaining 800 Bataan survivors. How would they ever get us all out in time?

February 5, 1945

The Americans moved 1,300 people from Bilibid Prison to the Ang Ti Bay shoe factory in one night. All of the Bataan soldiers plus our women and children were transported by truck. Those who could walk, including Harry, started out on foot and were picked up later on the second trip.

At the shoe factory, we got our first glimpse of the Bataan POWs—some without arms and legs, others mere skeletons, too weak to even walk. Some are mentally disturbed. Many are on stretchers. It's awful. We hear that the Japanese ship transporting the other 1,600 soldiers was sunk not far from Manila Bay. No survivors as far as we know.

February 6, 1945

A field kitchen is set up for us and we are served breakfast. Imagine! Oatmeal with real milk and white sugar, scrambled eggs and real ham and hot chocolate. What a feast! Lunch is creamed salmon and cold asparagus. Dinner—pork with gravy, Irish potatoes and mixed vegetables. Snacks include bread, butter, jam, cheese, canned fruit juice, sugar and milk. This new diet causes serious disorders of the stomach, however. I guess we need time to adjust.

February 8, 1945

We stayed at the shoe factory for only 24 hours. By then the fires have died down so we are taken back to Bilibid Prison for lack of a safer place. What a shock to find that everything has been looted.

The fight for Manila has gone on for some days. General MacArthur came to our prison today to assure us he would try his hardest to get us out of Manila soon.

We have been prisoners for more than 1,100 days. A lifetime, it seems! Especially with two small children. It is the goodness of the Lord that we are still alive to see liberation.

War continues around and above us, but we are free, surrounded by our own armed forces. GIs in fighting gear come into the protection of our prison walls for rest and regrouping before returning to the front lines.

February 14, 1945

Harry asked an Air Force officer why there had been no bombings on December 27th and 28th. Those were the two days we were being moved from Baguio to Manila. On our trip we had seen many Japanese troops and tanks moving north from Manila, but the daily forays of the bombers were curtailed on those days.

The officer stopped to think for a few minutes. "If there was no bombing, it was because there was no fuel in Leyte. Had planes been able to fly, the Japanese trucks transporting you would have been bombed off the roads." God had intervened and protected all of us in answer to prayer!

We have had word that the first U.S. Army repatriation plane will be ready shortly to fly Bilibid civilian internees to the island of Leyte. Manila harbor is full of sunken Japanese ships—it is impossible to use.

February 17, 1945

Chaplain Webster, an Alliance chaplain, invites Harry to drive down to New Bilibid Prison to visit the recently rescued Los Baños internees. While Harry is gone, his cousin, Bob Lane, who fought with the 1st Cavalry all the way from New Guinea to Manila, finally locates us. Unable to find us at first, he had sent a telegram to family in the States stating we weren't in Manila. How exciting to see him! It's too bad Harry missed his visit but Bob expects to come back again soon.

February 20, 1945

Yesterday, Bob came back. He took a picture of the four of us at the entrance to the prison.

Harry's tooth is causing him severe pain so he walked alone the several blocks to Santo Tomás University where a U.S. Army dental clinic has been set up. The young dentist said there was no way to save the tooth. The decision was "pull!"

The first attempt broke the tooth off at the gum. After a considerable amount of hammering and chiseling, the dentist said, "I can't find the roots. Go get an X-ray." When continued efforts failed, Harry was sent for a second X-ray. By the time he returned, the dentist had gone to lunch. Harry begged for another dentist to help. They were all first lieutenants, recent dental students. Not a big morale booster! But finally one agreed to do the job.

Can you believe it? In the midst of the extraction, orders came to transfer this dentist to a new location, so he laid down his tools, picked up his gun and left!

Harry was determined not to leave till someone came to his rescue. Thankfully, from somewhere, a dentist with rank appeared. The novocaine had unfortunately worn off and they decided against injecting more. The dentist took a corkscrew-type instrument and brought up all he could find. He then packed the hole with sulfa drug and told Harry to go.

Harry had to walk the half mile back to Bilibid Prison in the hot sun with an aching jaw. He could feel it swelling. Added to his own pain were the ravages of war and death evident everywhere.

When our camp internee dentist at Bilibid saw Harry's predicament, he said he only hoped our names would be drawn for the first plane out.

February 22, 1945

The drawing of 40 names for the first plane took place. We are not among them!

February 23, 1945

Trucks were to leave for the improvised airport at 11 a.m. A family of four on the list could not travel because one of the children had a high fever. The camp doctor came to examine Harry's swollen jaw and ordered us to be the replacement. Praise the Lord!

On our arrival in Leyte, the women and small

children were taken to one camp, the men and boys to another camp about 20 miles away. We were all issued army khakis.

March 2, 1945

Our ship is a naval transport, the *Admiral William Capps*, part of a naval convoy.

Women and children are placed in officers' quarters above deck. In the officers' mess we actually sit down at tables to eat!

The men's quarters are all below deck with the GIs. Harry is three decks below us. No portholes. The bunks are pieces of canvas attached to frames of metal piping and arranged in tiers of four. There are literally hundreds of them.

The men have their meals in the troop mess and have to wait in chow line for every meal. They eat standing up. Harry's jaw is less painful as pus works its way out of the opening.

March 23, 1945

We have sailed by convoy south to the Marianas to refuel and to pick up a new escort that will stay with us for two days. It will be rather frightening when the escort ship turns back. We are zig-zagging across the ocean to avoid Japanese submarines.

One day our ship developed engine trouble and we sat like dead ducks in the water for several hours. Scary!

Our children are loved and cared for by the soldiers on board. Don is delighted with all the food, but Janice can't digest it. We have had to resort to mostly tomato juice. It seems to agree with her.

March 30, 1945

It has been 28 days since we left the Philippine Islands. How can I express just how it feels to pass under the Golden Gate bridge? We are home! I remember my prayer when I was in Notre Dame Hospital: "Lord, it doesn't matter about our belongings. Just please get all four of us back to the States."

The 1,137 days of captivity are over at last! We can begin a new life.

Earl and Pauline Sexauer met us in San Francisco and took us to their home. They fed and clothed us for two weeks with the help of the folks from the Oakland Neighborhood Church (now Cathedral at the Crossroads).

As soon as it could be arranged Harry visited a dental surgeon who operated on his jaw. The remaining roots left in by the Manila dentist were extracted. The surgeon said, "There was enough infection there to kill 10 men." How great our Lord's mercy and care!

Finally, on April 15, 1945, we arrived at Harry's home in Pennsylvania. Dad Taylor showed us a clipping from the local newspaper dated January 4, 1943: "Rev. Harry Taylor and family reported well in Japanese camp. The parents received the first word in over two years. . . ." Harry's parents also received the 25-word message we had written in Camp Holmes and which was delivered via the Red Cross.

Soon after our arrival in the States a letter from my parents in Beirut, Lebanon, arrived. They were so relieved to hear of our release from the prison camp. God had given them a promise, Psalm 105:13–16. "They wandered from nation to nation, from one kingdom to another. He allowed no one to oppress them; for their sake he rebuked kings: 'Do not touch my anointed ones; do my prophets no harm.' "

God had kept this promise in a most unique way. He had answered prayer in His time.

Part III

Cambodia: Our People, the Khmer

*. . . how you turned to God from idols
to serve the living and true God, and
to wait for his Son from heaven. . . .
(1 Thessalonians 1:9–10)*

*A line of palms in the distance
and feathery tall bamboo
A brown man
A thatched hut
A lazy ole' caribou
While high above mountain and rice
    field
is the blue of heavens' dome
Some people call it Cambodia
Some people call it Home.*
        (Source Unknown)

10

Six Courageous Saints

(Harry and Miriam)

The people of Cambodia are unique among the peoples of Southeast Asia in that the culture is related to India. The Cambodian language is non-tonal. The national religion is Buddhism, which also came from India. Politically, the people of Cambodia traditionally follow India's neutrality and one of their basic foods is curry.

Cambodia is a rich agricultural area which produces a large percentage of Asia's rice crop. Its fruits are among the most delicious in the world. Hot tropical plains are crisscrossed by beautiful jade-colored rice fields, rich jungle forests abundant with hard woods and all kinds of wild game. The waters of Cambodia have the highest percentage of fresh water fish per square meter in the world. The western mountains shelter mines of precious stones. To the north are the ancient ruins of Angkor, considered by some to be one of the seven wonders of the world.

The French took over Cambodia as a protectorate in the 1800s. Though the Khmer had conquered and ruled a large part of Southeast Asia since the 14th century, reverses and defeat followed. To prevent being swallowed up by their neighbors, Cambodia requested France to make them a protectorate. It was from Cambodia that France went on to conquer Vietnam and Laos and to establish Indochina as a French colonial empire.

The French did a masterful job of developing the natural resources. Indochina's geographic position and resources helped to fire the expansionist vision of Japan that eventually brought World War II to Asia.

The French colonial effort also inspired extensive development in every area of Indochina, a factor which facilitated evangelization.

The Christian and Missionary Alliance was the first Protestant missionary society to penetrate the opposition of the French colonial government and begin mass evangelism in Vietnam. The French, at that time, refused to permit Alliance missionaries into Cambodia, claiming they were sworn to protect the national religion of Buddhism. They did, however, allow Catholic churches in every provincial center of the country and in smaller towns as well.

Through the prevailing prayers of God's people and the tireless efforts of Dr. R.A. Jaffray, the great missionary statesman, plus the persistence of the Arthur Hammonds, the David Ellisons and the Floyd Petersons, the tide turned. These three families courageously entered Cambodia. They translated the Scriptures, trained church leaders and evangelized the populace in spite of great opposition from religious leaders and the government.

Volumes could be written about these six courageous saints who blazed the trail into Cambodia. The 30 of us who followed were inspired by them to put our hands to the plow and trust God for miracles even as they had. We cherish their memory.

The Floyd Petersons, both of a joyful disposition and optimistic outlook, were given the responsibility of evangelism. They also held short-term Bible schools (now known as Theological Education by Extension—TEE) in the provinces.

Dr. Jaffray appointed Arthur Hammond, residing in the capital city of Phnom Penh, to translate the Bible into Cambodian. Hammond was a man of genius and courageous endurance—undisputed virtues for a translator who must not only understand the Word, but by sweat and tears find the foreign equivalent that will unveil the truths of God.

Toward the end of Arthur Hammond's years in Cambodia his eyesight was nearly lost from the long hours, days and years of translation and revision. Hammond not only translated the Bible but designed the special Cambodian type face used in its printing. This type, produced in France, was eventually used in Cambodia by the media and for other purposes.

Later on, due to the political unrest in Cambodia at the time, Arthur Hammond took the manuscripts to Nyack Missionary College. He, with the capable assistance of missionary Harold

Sechrist and a Nyack student, Cliff Westergren, taught the students to set the type. This colossal task was done by hand, word by word, page by page. The British and Foreign Bible Society in England printed the Bible. A specially bound copy, personalized in gold leaf, was presented to King Norodom Sihanouk soon after the project was completed.

Dr. Jaffray also appointed the David Ellisons to open a Bible school in Battambang, North Cambodia. The Bible school was vital to train leaders as congregations of believers began to emerge and multiply. The caliber of the preachers and teachers trained at the school was such that government officials expressed amazement at their unusual abilities. Even Catholic priests inquired about the school's training programs. They had not, they said, produced even one committed Cambodian priest in over half a century.

On one occasion I heard Brother Ellison pray: "Lord, after we have done our best we are but unworthy servants." In the early 1960s, David Ellison died of a massive heart attack as he was preparing to leave on an evangelistic trip. The body of this courageous missionary lies in the country he loved, awaiting the resurrection.

It was to this legacy of love, commitment and service and this beautiful country and gentle people that we were about to dedicate 18 more years of our lives.

11

Back to Cambodia

(Harry)

In 1947, after two years of post-war recuperation and the birth of our third child, Judith Esther, we returned to Cambodia and took up where we had left off in 1941. The story of the next 18 years is best told through the lives of our people—the Khmer.

Behind Bars

The provincial prison was located in the city of Kompong Cham. We often saw the work gangs as they labored on the roads or walked to their daily assignments in the hot sun, dragging chains attached to both legs.

To our knowledge, no prison in Cambodian history had ever opened its gates to a gospel witness. Could we incorporate a prison ministry into our plans for evangelizing this country?

One day, while visiting the governor of our province, I told him that I would like to have permission to hold weekly services in the prison. His reply was a flat refusal.

"Those prisoners are dangerous," he argued.

"They are no better than the dogs on the street. How can I grant permission for you to enter the prison?"

Fortunately, we had done several favors for the governor. On occasion I had acted as his interpreter for American aid projects. His son had also attended our Vacation Bible School sessions and had enjoyed the classes. I decided to press my advantage for a positive reply.

When the governor realized I was serious about the request, he began to weaken.

Finally he said, "You can enter the prison on one condition—you will take full responsibility for whatever may happen. We will open the gates, let you in, then close the gates behind you."

Without hesitation I replied, "Governor, that is exactly what I want. I will take full responsibility. Thank you."

We prepared the pump organ for Miriam to play. I would play my trombone. Two pastors were to go with us—a Cambodian and a Vietnamese.

The day for the first meeting arrived. We loaded everything in the car and drove off. The guards were prepared for us and immediately ushered us through the big front gates. They locked behind us. We were on our own. But we knew the Lord had gone before us in answer to prayer.

The guards helped us carry our instruments to the assembly room where they provided us with several chairs. With a puzzled expression on their faces the guards bid us goodbye. Once again, the iron gate slammed shut.

Soon several hundred prisoners marched in—

both men and women. They seemed shocked to see two Americans.

We sang several songs for them accompanied by our instruments. As we were trying to teach them some choruses, I glanced toward the gate. The guards were standing with their heads against the bars, listening in disbelief to the joyous singing of these condemned people. For a moment it seemed that we were on the outside and the guards were the prisoners. I talked about Jesus and His love for every person. Before we left we distributed Cambodian and Vietnamese New Testaments and Christian literature.

Sometime later, the king of Cambodia paid a visit to our station. He had come to Kompong Cham to greet the populace, to address the foreign residents and to present medals for service rendered for the good of the people. What a surprise when I was called to the platform to receive a medal.

Later, we were transferred to Phnom Penh and the prison services were terminated. But when visiting the province, we would often pass chain gangs on the road.

"Lok Taylor," they would shout out in greeting. *If they remember my name,* I thought, *maybe they remember my message, too.* I hoped so. Perhaps we would meet some of them in heaven some day.

A Nice Fat Lady

From the first days of authorized gospel ministry in Cambodia, government restrictions were very severe. The threat of expulsion from the country was constantly held over the heads of the missionaries. It was illegal to witness to the Cambodian public. The permission to do any evangelism applied only to the Chinese and Vietnamese of whom there were many in the country. In a short time, however, Cambodian believers in Christ began to multiply in spite of the fact that some were imprisoned for their faith.

The government eventually granted permission to preach to Cambodians, but only to confirmed Christians. The discrimination, direct and indirect, never did disappear but surface toleration became more and more relaxed.

After World War II, this kind of discrimination was soon overshadowed by the communist rebel bands which roamed the country, pillaging and killing. Their main aim, of course, was to force out the French government administration. At first glance, over the sights of a rifle, it was rather difficult to distinguish between a Frenchman and an American. One incident will illustrate just how tense the situation was.

Miriam and I were on an evangelistic trip with several Bible school students in northeast Cambodia where rebel bandits were active.

We drove into a marketplace and began to witness and pass out literature. As it was a very hot day, Miriam decided to stay in the car parked in the shade of a large tree. Several hours later I returned to the car to find her somewhat shaken.

"What's the matter?" I asked.

"A soldier stopped and asked me where we are headed," she replied. "I told him we intend to go

on up north to Kratie. He looked at me rather
strangely and said, 'I hate to see such a nice fat
lady like you get killed. If you go on that road, you
will likely be ambushed by rebels. Just yesterday,
17 French soldiers were killed on that very same
road. Certainly you will be killed too!' "

We knew that was a possibility. It was not unusual to see dead bodies floating down the river or
lying on the highways. What should we do? We
prayed and decided to go on as planned. There was
no ambush, and, praise the Lord, we finally arrived
safely in Kratie.

Yea'a Psa Suon

The woman's eyes were dull, her mind clouded,
her heart burdened down with a load she was not
able to bear. Yea'a Psa Suon was desperate. All her
fortune had been spent on mediums and sorcerers.
Worse yet, she had become demon-possessed. She
was so violent and strong she would wreck any
room in which she was locked.

One day, her son came to our Mission house and
headquarters where the executive committee was
in session. He pleaded for help. He had heard that
our God could cast out evil spirits.

"Will you come quickly and help us?" he
pleaded.

We broke off our meeting and drove to where the
woman was being held. A large, curious crowd was
waiting. My first inclination was to send them
away, then I thought, *They need to see what the Lord
can do.* They followed us to the garden where the
woman was seated in a chair. Obviously in a

trance, she was rigid, staring straight ahead with glassy eyes.

The five of us began to pray, pleading the blood of Christ and claiming the power of Jesus to undertake by the authority of His Word. Then we turned to Yea'a ("older woman") and commanded the spirit, "In the name of Jesus, come out."

No response. Only the same evil sneer.

We went back to prayer.

We turned to Yea'a a second time, but were met with the same negative response.

Then we commanded the evil spirit, "In the name of Jesus, give us your name."

"Prah Chan (moon god)," came the answer from Yea'a's mouth. But it was not her voice. This voice was deep, tortured, raspy.

We went to prayer for the third time. Opening our eyes, we noticed Yea'a moving her mouth in a strange way.

"Yea'a, open your mouth," I was impressed to command.

As she did so, a bright shiny object appeared. I reached in and pulled it out. It was a tiger's tooth. She had held it in her mouth for months at the instruction of a medium.

"In the name of Jesus, come out," we commanded once again. Immediately the weird, staring gaze was gone. Yea'a recognized us and began to converse.

The change was remarkable. Those who stood around watching were amazed to see the previously possessed woman released from the control of the evil spirits. She became alert and peaceful. Light came back into her eyes.

Someone in the crowd said, "We Buddhists bargain with the evil spirits by offering eggs or whatever is available and begging the spirits to come out. But you Christians command the evil spirits to come out in the name of Jesus and they obey."

We replied, "Yes, it is Jesus who has brought deliverance!"

The following day Yea'a appeared at our front door. What a joy to see her well, her eyes bright. But when she tried to speak, her voice was once again coarse and raspy.

"Every time I try to read my Bible," she said, "the evil spirits in my house try to choke me. You cast those evil spirits out of me. Now, please come and cast them out of my house."

Miriam and I took our Bibles and our song books and went with Yea'a back to her home—a big, old, wooden house that belonged to her once wealthy family.

We began by singing songs about the power of the blood of Christ. Then we read the Scriptures where our Lord commissioned His disciples to cast out evil spirits in the name and by the power of Jesus: "I am sending you to them to open their eyes and turn them from darkness to light, and from the power of Satan to God . . . " (Acts 26:17b–18a).

Then we prayed, "Thank You, Lord, for our dear sister who has turned from Satan to God. She belongs to You. Her house belongs to You, too. We plead the blood of Jesus to cover this house." To the evil spirits we said, "We command you in the name of Jesus to depart from this house and never return."

We looked up to find Yea'a with tears in her eyes. "I saw the evil spirits leave, weeping as they fled," she said.

Miriam and I saw nothing of which she was so familiar. But, praise God, we saw His wonderful deliverance for Yea'a and her home.

Princess Rasmey (Samdach Rea'smey Sophana)

Prince Norodom Sihanouk was reared from childhood by his unmarried aunt, Princess Rasmey ("rays of light"). When the prince became king, his children were considered to be the grandchildren of the princess. They went to school at the French Lycee Decartes where Nellie Guilbert, a dedicated believer, was the school nurse.

The princess and Nellie met often to discuss the health of the children. Their conversations sometimes included spiritual topics and Princess Rasmey became more and more interested in the gospel. She finally accepted the way of Christ but did not dare to declare it openly in the palace. It was through Nellie that we were introduced to the princess.

One day, when Nellie was visiting us, she mentioned that Princess Rasmey was soon to have a birthday. She asked us if we would be willing to have a party for her. It was a splendid idea. We sent the invitation to the princess, planned the meal and arranged everything as elegantly as possible. Our youngest daughter, Judy, home on vacation from Dalat, made the birthday cake—a three-tiered masterpiece, decorated with white frosting and cherries.

The hour finally arrived for the momentous occasion.

The princess, dressed in a colorful silk sampot with a shawl of silk over one shoulder, arrived in her black limousine. After visiting briefly in the living room, we proceeded to the dining room where the princess was seated in the place of honor at the table. Dinner was served by courses, French style.

After the appetizer, soup and fruit courses, Judy brought in the birthday cake, candles glowing. We all sang "Happy Birthday." The princess had never had a birthday cake before. She was visibly touched.

After we had eaten dessert, the princess rose to her feet at the head of the table.

"May I make a speech?" she asked.

Request granted, she began.

"We will ever be grateful that you came to our country. You have brought us joy with the message you present. May God protect you. If anyone attempts to do you harm, I will help you. We appreciate what you are doing for us here."

Chan Hom

Chan Hom was born into a Christian family in the rural rice-growing area of northern Cambodia. We knew Chan from his early childhood when he heard God calling him to become a pastor.

After Bible school, Chan went back to his own province which was already torn by unrest and bloodshed. The communist infiltration was pervasive.

He married Soun, also a Bible school student and they courageously ministered to the believers in his church and to the whole rural community. When the Khmer Rouge took over, the Christians were forced to hide their Bibles and song books. Chan wrapped his Bible in a plastic bag and buried it under his own house. After darkness fell each night, he would retrieve his precious possession. He knew he had to feed his own soul in order to minister to others.

Four years later, when the Vietnamese army invaded Cambodia, Chan Hom, his family and some of their fellow believers fled to Thailand. They were put in a refugee camp where 100,000 Cambodians were kept behind fences and guarded by the Thai army.

Chan began to hold services and preach the gospel in the camp. Thousands of Cambodians confessed their sins and expressed faith in Christ as Savior. Chan opened a Bible school in the camp to instruct those who had come out of the night of Buddhism. These believers have since scattered throughout the world.

Today, Chan Hom pastors a large Cambodian church in Long Beach, California. He has been able to take a trip back to Cambodia, an event he never dreamed possible.

Reach Yea and Kapho

Reach Yea, the son of a preacher, was sick in the hospital, having lost the use of one lung to tuberculosis. Nevertheless, he still wanted to serve the Lord. Yea was certainly gifted and intelligent, but he was so weak and thin that we wondered if he would live, let alone be able to attend Bible school and later endure the strenuous life of a pastor in Cambodia.

We prayed for him and Yea believed for his own healing. God responded to that faith and some time later Yea applied to go to Bible school.

Yea continued to gain strength. He studied hard and began to work with us on the radio programs which we sent to the Far East Broadcasting Company in Manila. These daily programs were beamed back into Cambodia. Reach Yea produced the scripts, preached and directed the dramatization of Bible stories with a cast of students from the Bible school.

Kapho was the daughter of a poor family who lived across the road from our Bible school. Their house was made of thatch (palm leaves), dried and strung on a stick to form a sheet. The thatched roof of Kapho's home had gaping holes. A new layer of thatch was needed to provide protection from the torrential tropical storms of the approaching rainy season.

But the family had no money.

There were many wealthy Chinese living in a village nearby. Why not go to one of these families and ask for a loan? But, as custom dictated, it would be necessary to leave something of value until the debt was repaid. What did the family have of value? It was decided that they would pawn their daughter, Kapho, to work off the debt.

One day Kapho arrived at our house, out of breath from having run from the village to the Bible school.

"I'll never be free—never, ever," she cried. "The Chinese family disapproves of everything I do. They keep adding to my parents' debt so they can keep me longer. Youth conference is coming soon and I want so much to attend. Please help me get free!"

That particular month we had received a gift of money with a note attached: "Use where most needed." Asking the Lord to make a way where there was none, we drove over to the village and found the Chinese family who had bought Kapho. They received us cordially and after several salutations we told them we had come with a proposition.

"We are interested in Kapho," we explained. "Youth conference starts soon and we would like Kapho to attend."

Before they could reply, we added, "Would you allow us to buy Kapho. We have a sum of money."

"How much do you have?"

We showed them, feeling ashamed to be transacting the destiny of a young girl with money.

"You may take her."

We could hardly believe our ears. It was a miracle.

Kapho came home with us. Janice was home for vacation from Dalat school and the girls became good friends. Kapho had a wonderful time at the youth conference, then she returned to her own family.

One night, as we were getting ready for bed, we heard loud voices. Harry lit the kerosene lamp and went out on the back porch. There stood some of our neighbors from across the road holding Kapho in their arms.

They laid her on the porch and we noticed that her leg was discolored and swollen. She was drifting in and out of consciousness.

"Kapho was walking along the road in the dark," someone explained, "and she stepped on a snake. It must have been a very poisonous one. See where the fangs penetrated her foot. Lok, help us! She is going to die!"

Harry dashed into the bathroom to get our first aid and snake bite kits. He painted the wound with disinfectant and cut a cross on the top of the foot. He then took a large syringe and began to suck out the poison. Turning to the parents he said, "We must rush her to the hospital."

The doctor on duty slashed the foot still deeper and continued to pump out poison. Kapho hung between life and death all that night as the Bible school students prayed. In the morning a telephone call informed us that she was still alive, but would have to stay in the hospital at least a month. God had answered our prayer. It was a great encouragement to all of us at the school.

The following year, Reach Yea and Kapho were married at the Bible school.

During the years of the holocaust in Cambodia we heard nothing about them. Refugees continued coming to America by the hundreds from the camps in Thailand, but no Reach Yea or Kapho. Because of their previous health problems we surmised they were dead.

Then, one day, my sister Evelyn phoned to say that Yea and his family had lived through the dreadful Pol Pot regime and were now in the United States.

12

God's 400

(Harry)

It was 1962. Only four students were enrolled at the Bible school. Was it worth the time, expense and effort to teach just four young men? It was a question that begged an answer.

The committee, of which I was a member, finally decided to praise God for the four promising young men who wanted to study and to keep the school open.

The students insisted on calling themselves "God's 400," a name that would engender courage in the face of the big task they hoped to do in reaching Cambodia for Christ.

Sok Prasar

Sok Prasar was a second year student. Although he had unusual zeal and talent for witnessing, he seemed unable to keep up with the other students.

Due to his penchant for joking and entertaining the other students, I often wondered if any Bible truths ever got through his head and down into his heart. Would he ever qualify as a Christian worker?

The Pol Pot regime determined to crush the elite,

to bring down the mighty and educated and to do away with Christians. Unfortunately, with guns and power it succeeded with the plan. Those with a fourth grade education or higher, those who wore glasses (a sign of being literate) and those with money and possessions were the main targets.

Night after night cadres knocked on doors, taking whomever they chose. We are told that a total of two million people were sent to their death. Not only adults were slaughtered but babies as well. Whole families were buried alive. Multitudes were dumped into mass graves. Piles of skeletons covered the fields and lay scattered in the forests and mountains.

Prasar, too, faced the terror of the Pol Pot regime.

"Do you proclaim to be a Christian?" his interrogators asked.

"Yes, I do."

"Do you know what we can do to you as a Christian?"

"Yes, I know full well what you can do to me."

"Do you intend to remain a Christian when we say we will kill you?"

"Yes."

"All right. If you continue to say you are a Christian, we will crucify you like they crucified your Jesus."

Prasar stood firm. So the Communists proceeded to perform the execution as they had threatened. Witnesses reported that Prasar surprised everyone by boldly saying, "I am not worthy to be crucified like Jesus. Crucify me upside down." His tormentors heeded the request and Prasar, along with one of his converts, was crucified upside down.

Pok Suor

The second member of God's 400 was Pok Suor.

Pok Suor was not able to get out of the country during the terrible reign of Pol Pot. However, we heard that he survived the holocaust and married the daughter of the Christian caretaker of the Bible school property.

San Hay Seng

In 1947, shortly after we returned to Cambodia for our second term, a young boy named San Hay Seng stood at our door.

"My grandmother is dying," he said. "We don't want to lose her. Could you come quickly and try to save her?"

We found the elderly woman lying on a mat with 20 or 30 members of the immediate family sitting on the floor, watching and waiting as the Buddhist incense permeated the house. Seng's grandmother was about to step into a Christless eternity without having heard the good news.

"Oh Lord," we prayed, "don't let these dear children die in hopeless ignorance like their grandmother."

We left.

That evening, as the sun was setting, we knew the inevitable had happened. The night air was filled with bitter wailing and the shrill gongs and drums of death.

After the Buddhist funeral I went to visit the grieving family. As I entered the house, I noticed that a cross had been placed on one of the wooden supports of the roof. On the cross hung a garment. Pointing to the cross, I asked, "Ta (Grandfather), what does this mean?"

The old man replied, "That cross protects us. The sweater belonged to my wife. I hung it there to prevent the evil spirits from coming back to make the rest of us sick."

I took the opportunity to tell him about the true meaning and power of the cross of Christ and then I left.

Several weeks later we held a Vacation Bible School. San Hay Seng and his cousin came. They both prayed to accept Christ as their Savior and Seng began attending church.

Seng's father was a silversmith who made idols of gold and silver, a very lucrative business. Now, to have his son believe in Jesus and follow the Christian belief made him uncomfortable. He threatened his son, but this only made Seng more sure than ever that he had chosen the right road.

After the VBS we made a list of the children who had made commitments and sent it to Ted and Dorothy Crane, our faithful prayer partners in Cranford, New Jersey. As they read the list they were particularly impressed to pray for two of the boys—San Hay Seng and Pen Dara.

Seng became the youth leader in Kompong Cham and after graduating from college was offered a job with the government. This meant a home, a car and a good future. I expected that Seng would be delighted with this new development. But when we met he looked sad.

"Mr. Taylor," he began, "I don't understand what

has happened. I know God called me to preach the gospel to my own people. Why has this good job been offered to me? Do you think God has opened up this opportunity so I can help support the pastors who are already serving the Lord? Do you think God might have changed His mind for me?"

I replied, "Seng, I can't answer your questions, but I can assure you of one thing—God has not changed His mind."

"If I turn down this job," Seng continued, "my father will disown me." (In Cambodia, the family security plan is fulfilled by the whole family backing the most promising children. When they get a good job, the mother and father go to live with the affluent offspring.) The call of Christ was cutting right across Seng's culture. What a struggle!

"Seng, if you obey the Lord," I said, "you will see His mighty power on your behalf. You will never be sorry."

The next time I saw Seng he was all smiles.

"Mr. Taylor," he beamed, "I have decided to obey my Savior regardless of what happens to me."

Seng's family did disown him and he had to trust God for the money to enter Bible school.

When Seng's mother was dying, we went with Seng to visit her in the hospital. We read the Scriptures and prayed. She knew that no one would have taken the step of faith her son had taken without the assurance that his God was real. She, too, accepted Christ.

As we were leaving the hospital, someone called. "Seng! Your mother has another question!"

"Son," she asked, "how am I going to know Jesus

when I see Him? Is He going to be dressed in white?"

Seng replied, "Mother, you don't need to worry. Jesus will be at the door of heaven to welcome you. He has prepared a place for you."

A few days later Seng's mother went to be with the Lord.

One day, Seng unexpectedly went home and found his father in deep thought. He had just finished forming an idol to sell. As he held it in his hands he said, "It is not right that I should worship something I have made with my own hands." He, too, accepted Christ as his Savior.

Seng became the director of the Bible school in Phnom Penh. He and his wife Hannah were sent to the Ebenezer Bible School in the Philippines to upgrade his training for Bible school leadership. While they were in the Philippines, Cambodia fell to the communists.

Seng and Hannah now live in the Los Angeles area and Seng has been appointed president of the Cambodian Takhmau Bible School, an extension of the school that the David Ellisons began in Cambodia years before.

Pen Dara

It was a lovely, fall Sunday afternoon in 1965 when the telephone rang at our home in Nyack, New York. We were on furlough from Cambodia, unable to return because our visas had not been renewed.

Pen Dara, the fourth member of God's 400, was on the line. What a surprise to hear that he was in the States! He came to see us that very day. We were to speak at the Sunday evening service in Cranford, New Jersey, where the Cranes lived— the couple who had prayed so faithfully for two of God's 400—San Hay Seng and Pen Dara.

"Dara," we said, "will you go to Cranford with us? We'll surprise the Cranes first and then share in the evening service."

The three of us took off for Cranford, just one hour away. We knocked on the Cranes' door. When the door opened, we said, "Do you know who this is?" pointing to Dara.

They knew right away who he was, for he looked just like his picture. Here before them was an answer to their prayers. I'll never forget the thrill of the moment.

Dara, by now, had mastered four languages— Vietnamese, Cambodian, French and English. Therefore, it was not difficult for him to obtain a job with Voice of America. In Washington, D.C., he met and married Legaya, a Filipina. Some time later, due to the large number of converts in the Cambodian refugee camps in Thailand, Dara and Legaya were sent there to begin Bible training courses. These new refugee believers were destined to be scattered to any nation of the world that would accept them or they would be returned to Cambodia. Either way, it was urgent that the Christians be instructed in the Word of God.

In 1982, while teaching in a Thai refugee camp, Dara was afflicted with cancer and had to return to the States for surgery. Three years later, he was elected president of the Cambodian Evangelical Church (C&MA) here in the States.

On March 7, 1985, just five weeks after he was discharged from the hospital following a gallbladder operation, Dara lost control of his car on a rain-slicked road. It tumbled down a steep cliff, landing in the top of a tree. The car was totaled, but miraculously, Dara lived.

Joe Kong

"When I was in Cambodia," Joe relates, "I was among the chief of sinners. As one of the top government officials and a part of the elite in my country, I was very proud of myself. I thought that a high position, honor, education and money would be enough in life. I did not need God. I lived for the flesh—idolatry, adultery, drunkenness. I hated Christianity.

"In 1975 my family and I were sent to Bangkok to represent the Cambodian government on the Mekong Committee, a technical agency of the United Nations. While we were still in Thailand, Cambodia fell into the hands of the communists.

"Several months passed while I waited for a policy from the new government. I received nothing. But I did learn that the killing of top government officials, high-ranking military officers and innocent people had begun. I decided to go to the United States where I had been trained as a forester at Oregon State University. I knew that my family and I were very fortunate to be alive.

"When we arrived in Oregon, I got a job with the Department of Forestry in Salem and we rented a house owned by one of the members of the Salem Alliance Church.

"The church was sponsoring a group of Cambodian refugees who were mostly new believers. I was invited to go to church and I attended Sunday school with the Cambodians. The teaching was in English, then translated into French and finally into Cambodian. It was a tiresome process for all concerned.

"I volunteered to interpret directly from English into Cambodian. Everybody was relieved and I became the official interpreter for the Sunday school class.

"The Lord began to speak to me as I interpreted the Word of God. One night, Rev. Eugene Hall, a former missionary to Cambodia, came to my house and shared the gospel with me. That evening I knelt down and became a new creature in Christ. I realized then that it was by God's divine providence that I was spared from the 'killing fields' so that I could come to know Him."

In 1985 Joe Kong was elected to the Board of Managers of The Christian and Missionary Alliance.

When the Elephants Fight

When Norodom Sihanouk, the prime minister and dictator of Cambodia, saw his country being threatened and overrun by communist rebels, he envisioned Cambodia's fate to be "division and subjugation" like he had witnessed just over the border in Vietnam. It seemed it was always the pro-western countries that were under attack and being swallowed up.

So Sihanouk made a secret agreement with China to reject the free world, principally the United States, and give the communists, especially the Viet Cong, sanctuary in his country. This was intended to placate the communists and leave the Cambodian government and people unmolested. Sihanouk's frank appraisal of the political turmoil was: "When the elephants fight, the mice get out of the way."

In 1965, all Americans, including our family, were put out of Cambodia.

In 1972, Prince Sihanouk's pro-communist leanings were rejected by the populace in a free election. Sihanouk was replaced by a democratic government with General Lon Nol as president and the door was opened for a phenomenal response to the gospel.

The number of churches in the capital city of Phnom Penh alone grew from two to 28, with some reporting attendances of as many as 1,500. This all happened in just three short years before the Khmer Rouge, led by Pol Pot, took control and unleashed the Cambodian holocaust.

Part IV

Lebanon: A New Ministry, A New People

Not by might, nor by power, but by my Spirit, says the Lord of Hosts—you will succeed because of my Spirit, though you are few and weak. (Zechariah 4:6, TLB)

13

Sami

(Harry)

We arrived in Lebanon in September 1966. I had been appointed board representative by our denominational headquarters, with administrative oversight of Lebanon, Syria and Jordan. I also did some preaching through interpreters in the Arab churches throughout the area.

Although I enjoyed this ministry, my deepest desire was to pastor a local congregation. After much prayer and searching, the Lord led me to start an International Church in Beirut City. My in-laws, George and Lola Breaden, had conducted services in English during World War II. When the Breadens retired just two months after our arrival in Lebanon, all ministry was carried on in Arabic.

We were the only Alliance missionaries in Lebanon at the time. We had no building and had made only a few friends. One thing we did know, however, was that God had led us there.

"Lord," we prayed, "how do we do it? Where do we start?"

It was clear we had only one choice—we would

begin in our own apartment located on the edge of a Muslim area. Although the prospects were not very promising, we passed out invitations announcing services the following Sunday.

On Thursday, a knock came at our door. It was an elderly gentleman looking for a Seventh Day Adventist missionary. I had no idea who this person was or where he might live, but I offered the visitor a book, one of A.B. Simpson's, that had been translated into Arabic. I also invited him to come to our Sunday service.

"I'll be sure to come!" he assured me. In some cultures, people often tell you what they think you want to hear rather than what they intend to do. So I was not at all sure that the man would be there. But we asked the Lord to bring him back.

Sunday came and much to our surprise the elderly gentleman appeared with his wife and two granddaughters from Iran. By their name—Gemayal—I knew that they belonged to one of the top 25 families of Lebanon. In addition to the four of them, there were people of several other nationalities present also. This certainly was an international church!

One of the attendees, a young British woman, was the most uptight person I can ever remember meeting. She had been a follies girl, starting in Las Vegas and dancing her way around the world and eventually arriving at the famous Casino of Beirut. Shortly thereafter she met a Lebanese, married him and showed up in our first service!

I noticed she was very uncomfortable. She couldn't wait until the meeting was over so she could get outside for a cigarette. The minute the benediction was pronounced, she made a beeline for the door. But I beat her to it and was able to greet her as she rushed out. I never expected to see her again.

The next Sunday, however, Dorothy was back and seemed more interested than ever. At the close of the service she sought the Lord for salvation. We urged Dorothy to stay for lunch so we could get acquainted.

After we ate, Dorothy began to pour out her fears and concerns to us.

"My husband has put my suitcases out in the hall and has told me, 'It is finished. Go back to England,' " she blurted.

"Dorothy," I replied, "I know one thing. If you let Christ into your life and home you will find some answers." She seemed responsive. Then I startled her by saying, "Dorothy, take us to meet your husband."

Although she was somewhat reluctant, we got in the car and Dorothy directed us to her apartment house. A rickety elevator tugged us up to the fourth floor. As we stepped into the corridor, I said, "Dorothy, after we meet your husband, casually invite us to come over for dinner tomorrow night."

Dorothy looked concerned.

"I'm afraid of what my husband will do. I don't know if he will even come out to meet you. He's just come back from a flight and is probably tired."

We waited in the living room while Dorothy proceeded to the bedroom and announced our presence. A few minutes later, much to our surprise, a large, affable Lebanese appeared. He greeted us cordially. As we talked, he started to complain about his wife.

"You know, that wife of mine is impossible. I fly to Bombay, Bangkok, Saigon and bring back the most delicious fruit and she won't even open one up to see what they are like inside."

"Khalil, your troubles are over," I smiled. "Let us eat some of that fruit and while we eat we'll get acquainted." My mouth had been watering for a long time for a taste of tropical fruit!

We had a most congenial visit. As we were leaving, Dorothy said, "Khalil, let's invite the Taylors over for supper tomorrow night."

"That's a great idea!" he answered. "I'll cook the meal." Miriam promised to bring the dessert.

The next evening we were back at the Chaya home. Khalil was a very good cook and with Miriam's dessert the meal was complete.

Following dinner, we went into the living room. I gave Dorothy and Khalil each a New Testament and we had a Bible study. Before the evening was over the two of them were kneeling at their couch with their arms around each other crying, "Oh God, have mercy on us."

Dorothy, we soon found out, was a key person that God had brought our way. The ramifications for God and His kingdom could not even have been predicated.

One day Dorothy said, "I know a couple that I think you can help. They are like us—a British/Lebanese combination. They need your counsel."

"Okay, Dorothy," I answered, "set up a tea and invite them over so we can meet them and get acquainted."

Dorothy did just that. We somehow knew that this would be no ordinary tea. In fact, it turned out to be very special.

We were the first to arrive. When the doorbell rang again, in walked Joy Dagher and her son Paul, about 15 months old. Joy was one of the most beautiful British girls we had ever seen. She was also dressed elegantly.

Joy said, "My husband, Sami, has to work today." That was true, but what she didn't tell us was that Sami had told her to go check out the Taylors. If they were all right, he would meet them later. He hadn't worked in a hotel for 15 years for nothing!

We sought and received an invitation to visit the Dagher home. When we arrived, we found that Joy had fallen and broken her foot which was now in a cast. Sami was home taking care of her.

"Mr. Taylor," Sami exclaimed, "we have read some of the Bible, but we don't understand it." Maybe Sami didn't know it, but for a preacher, that was a most welcome invitation!

"Would you like to have a Bible study?" I asked. Joy and Sami agreed.

At the first session, Sami excused himself saying he was going to the bakery to get some sweets for tea. He was gone a long time and when he finally returned he was surprised to find us still waiting. He had expected us to be gone. He was not used to such persistent people! *Surely,* he thought, *they must have ulterior motives.*

We visited the Daghers between the regular study times. We helped them paint their apartment. Sometimes we went on picnics together. Miriam would often visit Joy with some sewing to do while they talked. At other times she would take over some baked goodies.

The day finally came. It was evident that the Holy Spirit, through the Word, was doing His convicting work in the Daghers' hearts. Joy sat with her Bible open on her lap, tears running down her cheeks.

"Mr. Taylor," she asked, "do you mean to tell me that if I take Christ as my Savior, I will never have to face my past again?"

I answered, "Joy, that is just what the Word of God tells us. Christ came to reconcile the world to Himself, not to count men's sins against them. If anyone is in Christ, he is a new creation. The old has gone, the new has come. All this is from God, who reconciles us to Himself through Christ. God made Christ, who had no sin, to be sin for us so that we could be righteous" (paraphrase of 2 Corinthians 5:17–21).

Joy's face broke out in a beautiful smile of relief. It was like the sun appearing from behind dark clouds. She threw her arms up in the air and shouted, "I am so happy I could tell the whole world!"

Sami prayed the prayer of repentance at that same time, too, but some stubborn vices put him through several very deep trials.

Sami was the manager and maitre d'hotel in the coffee shop of the largest and most prestigious luxury hotel in the Near East—The Phoenicia. He made good money and enjoyed the life of that glittering world.

But Sami had made a commitment and he became a very apt Bible student after he was saved. He read the Bible in three languages and he could speak five. He would often get home at midnight and read his Bible until two o'clock in the morning. His questions at our Bible studies were insightful.

About that time a millionaire from Australia stopped off at The Phoenicia. He immediately took a liking to Sami and invited him to go to Sidney to set up a ritzy restaurant there. They would share the profits, he said.

What a temptation! Sami had visions of gold. All else seemed to fade in the thrill of what might come to pass. In spite of our conviction that this was the devil's temptation, Sami determined to go. He could not think of anything else. However, in answer to our prayers and the grace of God, the deal fell through, as did many other similar temptations that confronted Sami on the way to victory in Christ.

Sami would often take his Bible studies to the hotel and give them to the employees who worked under him. All went well until one day a young man stood up and said, "Sami, your words are beautiful, but we don't buy it. What is the difference between you and us? We drink. You drink. We smoke. You smoke. Our stories are shady. Your stories are shady." With that they all got up and left the room. Sami was devastated.

That afternoon, Joy phoned us in a panic.

"Come quickly," she said. "Sami says he is throwing over his faith and he's going back into the world." Miriam and I headed for the Daghers.

We found Sami on the floor with perspiration pouring down his face. He was crying out in agony, "I don't deserve one single bit of God's grace. I am a hypocrite. I am going back into the world where I belong and serve the devil." Sami had finally come to the cross and discovered that we don't live the Christian life the way we want to live it. A revolution was about to take place in his life.

We had a prayer meeting that afternoon that we will never forget. It was a "battle royal" with the devil. But praise God, the Lord brought Sami through victoriously and filled him with the Holy Spirit.

We had a new Sami.

Not long after Sami's victory, a Lebanese evangelist came to me and pleaded, "Now that Sami is right with God, you had better get him out of that hotel. It's a wicked place down there."

I told him that I hadn't put Sami in that hotel and it wasn't my place to take him out. When Christ saves a man, He also keeps him and leads him in the decisions to be made. Sami was in God's hands.

The George Breadens, Beersheba, 1924. Miriam, front right.

Miriam grinding wheat with helper. Marjorie, right rear; Evelyn, left rear.

Miriam Breaden, age 15.

Below: Harry, Miriam and David, age 2, when they first arrived in Cambodia.

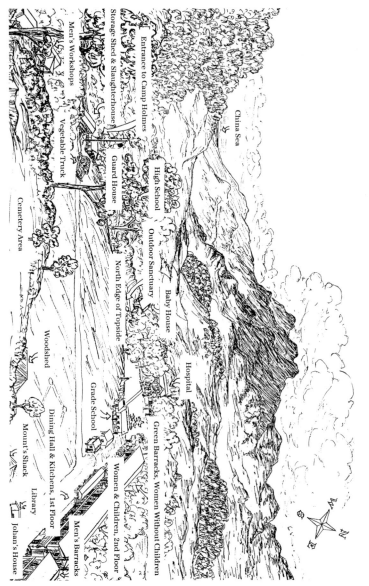

PANORAMIC VIEW OF CAMP HOLMES FROM THE "HILL"

China Sea

Men's Workshops

Storage Shed & Slaughterhouse

Entrance to Camp Holmes

Vegetable Truck

Guard House

High School

Cemetery Area

Outdoor Sanctuary

North Edge of Topside

Baby House

Woodshed

Hospital

Grade School

Green Barracks, Women Without Children

Mount's Shack

Dining Hall & Kitchens, 1st Floor

Women & Children, 2nd Floor

Library

Men's Barracks

Johan's House

Ruth Culpepper's Cubicle, June 1943

Co-mingling across the double fence. 1942

Mothers and children, taken in Bilibid Prison, 1945. Marian Gray's husband did not return from interrogation. To "compensate," the Japanese had a photographer take this picture.

The Taylors on the steps of Bilibid Prison, February 1945.

Kompong Cham Prison.

Ready to return to
Cambodia, 1947.

Harry and Miriam on their
25th anniversary.

Missionary staff in Cambodia, 1962.

Sami and Joy Dagher, 1970.

The International Church, Beirut, Lebanon.

Harry and Miriam with Natasha Rehani, 1978.

Beirut Ladies' Outreach Luncheon, 1972.

Rev. and Mrs. George Breaden after retiral in 1966.

Kra Reach Yea and Kapho, the girl the Taylors "bought" in Cambodia.

Hay Seng San, now the Director of Takhmau Bible School in California.

Dara Pen and Legaya.

The Taylors, in charge of the Takhmau Bible School
near Phnom Penh, 1952-1955.

Tour group in Jerusalem to celebrate the centennial of Alliance ministry, 1990.

14

A New Church, A New Leader

(Harry)

We hadn't the slightest idea how God could work out our problem. We had searched up and down the streets in Ras Beirut, the main section of Beirut where the embassies and large hotels are located, for a suitable meeting place to rent. There was nothing available.

Our congregation was growing. We had started services in our apartment with just a few people. Then we had moved the meetings to a larger home. Now, we were using a Christian school auditorium, but it, too, was only a temporary arrangement.

We had people but no adequate place to worship. Moving from place to place did not project permanency. We needed a facility where we could grow. Though we had no money, we prayed for an evangelistic center. But nothing was available and it seemed all the possibilities had been exhausted.

One day, as Miriam and I sat in the living room pondering the problem, the telephone rang.

"This is Dr. Fairbanks," the voice on the other end announced.

"Yes, what can we do for you?" I asked. I knew Dr. Fairbanks. A professor at Hagazian College, he had just started attending our services. I also knew that he was involved with Intervarsity.

"I am calling to inquire if you would be interested in renting a meeting place on Abdul Aziz near the American University. The Brethren group has met there for the past 12 years, but have now decided to give it up. The first floor is available for rent. They must know immediately."

Within two weeks, on Easter Sunday, we had our first meeting in the new facility. What a day of rejoicing!

A year later we purchased the three-story building. Half of the money was a gift from two special friends and the balance came from the Alliance Women of the United States and Canada.

The first floor provided a church auditorium, classrooms, offices, kitchen and bathroom facilities. The second and third floors were apartments which were already rented out. We needed one of the apartments to live in, but it was next to impossible to buy out a renter. In Beirut, renters have squatters' rights. Another seemingly impossible situation!

One day we drove over to the new facility and were astounded to see the top left apartment empty. What had happened?

We found out that serious animosity had developed between the two families occupying the top floor. The situation had become so unbearable that one family had moved out. Had they heard that we had bought the building they would have waited and demanded money from us.

It all happened so fast, but we knew it was another miracle! Now we had a wonderful new facility for our growing congregation and an apartment for us, too.

Temptation

One Sunday on their way to church the Daghers were discussing tithing.

Joy said, "Sami, we should start tithing to help support the Lord's work."

"Yes, of course," Sami replied, "but we have some debts to pay. When we have paid all our debts, we will begin to tithe."

That morning we had a visiting speaker. Can you guess what his sermon was about? Yes, he preached on tithing. All through the message Sami was mentally accusing Joy of telling the speaker about their discussion.

After the service, Sami turned to his wife, "Joy, did you tell that man to preach on tithing?"

Surprised, Joy answered, "I haven't even spoken to him." Then Sami knew that God was speaking through this visiting pastor directly to his own heart.

On the way home, Sami gave his tithe to Joy to put with the Sunday offering. It was a difficult step, for the rent was due and the Daghers had no other money on hand.

That very week, an unbelieving acquaintance became convicted about a nine-year-old debt he owed Sami. Knocking at Sami's door, the man paid what he owed. It was more than enough to pay the rent.

This was just the beginning of the Daghers' life-style of giving—giving of their money, giving of their love and giving of their lives in service for the glory of God.

Although Sami often had to work on Sunday, the hotel gave him two hours off to go to church. I never knew who Sami would bring along with him. It was his habit Sunday mornings to look around the dining room for anyone who might want to go to church. One morning he invited the Jennings Rowlands. They were active in our church for eight years while Mr. Rowland worked for Goodyear. He later became a member of the staff at Toccoa Falls College.

Many wonderful events took place in the hotel through Sami's testimony. But the devil was also busy. Sami's enemies reported him to the authorities for his witness—he had given tracts to some Russian visitors.

Another time, a wealthy woman approached Sami in tears. "Sami," she begged, "if you will go with me, I will take you anywhere in the world you want to go and get you anything you ask for. Just go with me. You will have no more earthly needs unmet." Without a word, Sami turned his back and walked away.

Another Temptation

A group of Christians from America discovered Sami's radiant testimony in the restaurant and asked him to leave the hotel and head up their newly proposed Mission to evangelize the villages of Lebanon. They would give him a car, a home and a salary comparable to the wages at the hotel if he would sign up with them.

The Lord had been speaking to Sami about full-time service. He certainly wanted to be all out for Christ. But later, Sami told me how he answered these men. "You have the wrong end of the stick. It would be better if you sent out your own missionaries and let them win converts. These converts could evangelize. Today, there are many who are willing to accept your money, but when you get through you will have nothing to show for it." Sami's words proved to be prophetic.

One day Sami came to me and said, "Mr. Taylor, God has been telling me for two years now to get out of the hotel. What shall I do?"

"Sami," I answered, "if you step out to serve the Lord Jesus Christ full time, remember, you will have to live on what the church can give you. That will be a far cry from your present hotel wages. But if God says 'go' you go. He has all the resources of heaven to take care of you. Just be sure you are hearing from Him."

To confirm the Lord's leading, Sami took his family up to a hotel in the mountains and left them there for three days while he gave himself to prayer. He told us to come to the hotel on the third day, have dinner with them and he would announce his decision.

When we arrived all we had to do was look at Sami's face. We knew what he had decided.

"God says 'go' and I am going to go," he beamed. We praised God, for we had prayed that Sami would one day become our associate pastor at the International Church.

No Severance Pay

Sami called the hotel management together and read his resignation. The owner was furious. He knew that the administration of the new Holiday Inn next door had been "fishing" at The Phoenicia for trained men and promising a larger salary. The boss imagined Sami was following the route other employees had already taken.

"Sami, what are you going to do?" he questioned.

Sami replied, "You know that some time ago the Lord Jesus saved me. He has changed my life and I don't have time to work here any more. I am going out to preach Christ all the time."

The owner of the hotel asked the obvious: "Sami, who is going to take care of you?"

Without hesitation, Sami answered, "God is going to take care of me!"

While the owner was recovering from that unexpected answer, one of Sami's fellow managers stood up and shook his finger under Sami's nose.

"Sami, the day will come," he blurted, "when you aren't going to have anything to feed your family. Don't you come to me, for I won't give you even one single crust of bread."

Sami stood firm.

The director and part-owner, thinking he would take the wind out of Sami's sails, shouted, "All right, Sami, you can go but we will give you no severance pay."

Sami had been counting on that severance pay to take care of his family while he got some schooling to prepare to become our associate pastor. For years money had been taken out of his paycheck and supplemented by the hotel. What a blow!

Suddenly, Sami turned to the hotel owner and exclaimed, "Sir, I don't care what you do. The Lord God of heaven has called me to serve Him. He is going to take care of me. Furthermore, if you don't pay me what you owe me, God will take care of you, too."

The owner was shaken. Finally he spoke. "Sami, we will give you your severance pay."

Less than three years later, during hand-to-hand fighting in Beirut City, the owner of The Phoenicia was killed in his own hotel.

Ordination

Sami got some schooling and the day was set when he would be ordained to the ministry. But who could foresee all that would take place on that momentous day?

There was heavy fighting in Beirut. The congregation of Sami's church in Karentina, on the east side of the city, didn't want to risk crossing over the Green Line (the demarcation line that ran north and south through the city) to the west side where the International Church was located.

So we decided to have two services. The ordination service would be held in the morning in Sami's church. A second service of celebration would be held in the afternoon at the International Church on the west side, preceded by a noon meal for any who were willing to risk the crossing.

Miriam stayed at the International Church with the Alliance Youth Corps team that had arrived only a few days before. I drove over to Karentina to take part in the ordination service.

The devil tried to hinder us at every turn. That very morning, someone attempted to blackmail Sami by putting a note in his car: "Unless you give me 70,000LL [Lebanese pounds] out of the relief funds, I will kill your wife and children." This was no empty threat! In those days of escalating war there were guns everywhere. However, after committing it to the Lord, we ignored the note and proceeded with the service as planned.

Then another distressing event took place. The soil pipe in the chapel ceiling began to leak onto the aisle carpet. There was nothing we could do. This unsavory drip continued throughout the entire service, then stopped. It has never leaked since that day.

The fighting in Beirut was so intense that only Sami, his family and a few others came to the service on the west side. Once again, as we were having refreshments on the patio, gunfire broke out. The visitors ran to their cars and hurried home.

Despite all the testings, Sami's ordination celebrations were marked by the unusual presence of the Lord, a sign from Him of things to come.

15

Miracles for Sami, Chawki and Ali

(Harry)

During a particularly fierce conflict, Joy Dagher and their two children went to England to visit Joy's parents. One of those days, while his family was gone, Sami answered a knock at the door.

He was surprised to see one of the managers from The Phoenicia, the one who had told him never to come to him for help—not even for a crust of bread. Sami welcomed him in and they discussed old times until there didn't seem to be anything more to talk about. Sami had many things to do and thought the guest would never leave.

Finally, the man got up and went out the door toward the elevator. He froze.

"Is something wrong?" Sami asked. "Do you need anything?"

The man answered, "Sami, I don't have anything to feed my family—not even a crust of bread." Sami ushered him back into the apartment and filled a basket from his own cupboard.

Later, Sami raised some money to send this same man to work in the big Riyadh Inter-Continental Hotel in Saudi Arabia. After his financial situation turned around, the man wrote Sami. "I want to thank you for what you did for me. I am sending you remuneration for helping me when I was in need."

Sami wrote back. "I won't accept any money from you. What I did for you, I did for Jesus. If you want to send some money to my church to help the needy, fine, but I won't take any for myself. And one more thing—if you don't repent of your sins and believe in Christ as your Savior, you will never, never make it."

Kidnapped!

The two men on the motorcycle obviously meant business. So, Sami Dagher, pastor of the Alliance Church in Karentina, Beirut, pulled his vehicle to the side of the mountain road. (One does not argue with guns in volatile Lebanon!)

Sami was on his way from Beirut to a church meeting in the mountains. He had lived long enough under the tensions of strife-torn Lebanon to recognize that an ominous situation was developing.

One of the two men climbed into the car beside Sami, pointed his gun menacingly and ordered him to drive. Leaving the main road, they made their way to an isolated area graced only by a solitary building. The kidnappers pushed Sami into a room. The door slammed shut and locked behind him.

Overpowering fear gripped Sami's heart. He

knew full well that these men were killers. They had stripped him of the car keys and all his papers, even his important identity card. He tried to pray, but the fear would not let go. He felt weak and totally helpless. He imagined his wife and children weeping after hearing of his death.

Suddenly he remembered his New Testament, still in his side pocket. His captors had somehow missed it. As he read, the Lord seemed to be speaking: "Do you want to go and be with Christ?" Sami was rather surprised by the question, but he also felt an indescribable joy and peace. Every earthly tie and attraction dropped away. His heart was filled with the Lord's presence.

An hour later the door opened and Sami was ordered into another room. Three men were waiting for him.

"Your name?"

"I am Sami."

"What is your occupation?"

"I am a servant of the Lord Jesus."

Surprised, his inquisitors asked, "If you are a priest, why don't you wear a clerical collar?"

"Why should I wear a clerical collar? I am ready to suffer with the rest of the people. You would not have taken me if I had been wearing a clerical collar."

"It is true," one of them replied, "and I guess there are some evangelical clergymen who don't wear collars."

Shortly, an older, distinguished looking man entered the room. The interrogators jumped to their feet and saluted.

Sami seized the moment.

"You may ask me any questions about Christ, the church, my family. I will answer nothing else. I know nothing else." He then told them how Christ had saved him from his sins. The men left.

Back in the locked room, Sami waited to see what would happen next. Some time later the door opened and a guide led him to the rear of the building.

"We are letting you go," the man said.

"Oh, no," Sami exclaimed. "I won't go like this. I won't leave until I have seen the other men again and am able to shake their hands."

Reluctantly, the others reappeared. They shook hands and presented Sami with his papers and car keys.

"We must have some coffee together, a sign of friendship," one of his captors offered.

"I can delay no longer," Sami countered. "I have a church service in a few minutes. But I will return at a later time and have coffee with you."

With that, he took his leave, praising God for deliverance and wondering who might have been praying for him.

Sami did return as he had promised to the isolated building in the mountains. Over a cup of coffee, he witnessed to his former captors and gave each of them a Bible.

Twice Saved

One night, while Sami's family was in England, he noticed that the streets were particularly quiet. For many months the Dagher family had been sleeping on floor mats in the hallway near the elevator. Several walls protected them there. But on this particular night, Sami decided to sleep in the bedroom since he didn't hear any shooting.

The Daghers lived on the sixth floor of a six-story building. The apartment block next door had only five stories plus a large iron cross on the roof.

In the middle of the night rockets began criss-crossing the city. Sami's neighbor saw one of the rockets heading straight for Sami's bedroom. On the way, however, it hit the cross on the roof next door and exploded, never reaching the Daghers' apartment.

When Sami's neighbor told him what had happened, he replied, "Praise God! I've been saved twice by the cross—first, when I accepted the Christ who died for me on a cross, and tonight when another cross intercepted a rocket that was headed for my bedroom."

Chawki

Across the hall from our apartment in the Mar Elias section of Beirut lived the Abbas family. Though not Christians, they were very open and congenial.

One afternoon, we came home and found Chawki, a high school student, sitting on the stairs by his apartment. He said he had no key and that he was waiting for his family to come home. We invited him into our apartment. After we chatted a bit to get better acquainted, I cautiously asked him if he knew anything about the good news of the gospel. He surprised me by saying that someone had given him a Bible and that he had already started to read it. I suggested we have a Bible study together.

"Great," he said, "I'll be glad to study with you."
Chawki not only came himself, but he brought
several of his Muslim friends with him. Later, at a
weekend youth conference sponsored by Youth for
Christ, Chawki made a public confession and accepted Jesus as his Savior.

When the Muslim leaders heard what had
transpired with Chawki, they became angry and
went to his parents, demanding that their son stop
going to the evangelical church. His parents were
perplexed. They were pleased with the change in
Chawki's life but they did not really understand the
significance of it. They told Chawki to discontinue
what he was doing or they would not pay for further education.

What a blow! Chawki was a good student and
wanted to eventually obtain his doctorate in
biochemistry.

Chawki no longer appeared at the church. Weeks
later, when our paths crossed, I asked Chawki
about his absence. He told us what had happened,
then added, "Don't worry about me. I am still a
believer. In another year I will be going to the
States to college and I'll be able to attend church as
I please." We were greatly relieved.

Chawki did pursue his studies in America. He
married Teresa, an American girl who was studying
to be a lawyer. They are both living for the Lord.

Ali

Ali, a handsome young Lebanese, born in Beirut,
was caught up in the struggles of his country. His
six brothers were also involved in the conflict.

Ali was the youngest in his family and had been

sent to Teheran for military instruction. The Ayatollah himself had challenged the young people to give all of their strength to the struggle to overthrow any opposition.

When Ali returned to Lebanon a meeting was held to decide who should drive a truckload of dynamite on a suicide mission to blow up a certain embassy in Beirut. No one volunteered. Feeling very brave, Ali raised his hand. To die for Allah would be a privilege.

Days passed. Ali was working as a waiter in the Summerland Hotel on the waterfront. It was situated not far from the embassy in question. The leaders decided that Ali would not be the one to blow up the embassy because he could be of more use to them at the hotel. Anyone who might escape death when the embassy was blown up would most likely go to the hotel for refuge. Ali's instructions were to be there to poison the food of any survivors.

A young man named Samir also worked at the hotel. Because of Sami Dagher's burden for the souls of the young men who worked in the hotels of Beirut, Samir had become a Christian. Samir's life took on new meaning. There were no more wild parties, no more drinking.

One day, Samir was swimming at a beach south of Beirut. It was a very windy day. He suddenly realized he was being carried out to sea and was rapidly losing the battle against the wind and waves.

Samir cried out to God, "Don't let me die here. No one will know what happened to me. I haven't witnessed to my parents about Christ yet. If You save me, I will go home and tell them about You."

On the highway above the beach, in a bus loaded with people, a man saw Samir's arm waving above the water. He asked the driver to stop the bus. He rushed down the cliff, dove into the water, swam out and saved Samir's life.

True to his promise, Samir went home and told his parents about his rescue from certain death and how God had changed his life.

Ali watched Samir day after day and noticed that he didn't smoke, drink and carouse. He was always composed, considerate and kind. He didn't get mad and curse. Ali couldn't understand such behavior.

One day he got up enough courage to ask, "Samir, why are you so different? We are both Muslims, born in Beirut. Both of us have been caught up in this horrible conflict. What is your secret?"

"Ali," Samir responded, "the secret of my life is this—I have accepted Jesus Christ as my personal Savior."

Ali was surprised, but he was also very angry. He told his Muslim friends about Samir and together they decided to do away with him. Ali gave them Samir's schedule and they promised to lay in wait for him.

But God was caring for Samir. He did not leave the hotel at his usual hour on that particular day. The attackers' plans were foiled. But Samir didn't come to work the next day or the next. What had happened? Where had he gone? Had he become suspicious, Ali wondered?

It was time for the destruction of the embassy. Ali had his particular job to do, but the more he thought about it, the more he knew he just couldn't go through with it. What should he do? How could he get out of it?

He made a quick decision to buy a ticket for Riyadh, Saudi Arabia. He would surely find work down there. Experienced waiters were always needed in hotels. And so he went. But who should be there ahead of him but Samir!

Ali couldn't believe it! Not only were Samir and Ali fellow-waiters again—they were roommates, too!

In Riyadh, Ali continued to watch Samir's life. How did it happen that Samir was so efficient and consistent in his actions, when he himself was in constant trouble, even being threatened with dismissal because he lacked self-control and good work habits? Ali wanted to be different, but he couldn't. He knew he had to change or he might be sent back to Beirut.

Again, he asked Samir to tell him what made him so different. "Ali, when I can trust you, I will tell you what makes me different."

Some time later Samir approached Ali. "I think I can trust you, now. I am willing to tell you my secret. I will need three hours. We will have to find a place away from other people."

"Why will it take three hours to tell me your secret?"

"It may take more than three hours," Samir responded.

Ali and Samir decided to meet at the International Airport. There would be no listening devices there, and, with the people coming and going, they would be able to talk in peace.

At the airport, Samir handed Ali a New Testament and they read the Sermon on the Mount together. While they were reading, Ali was comparing the words of the Bible with what he had been taught. He had been taught to curse, but Jesus spoke blessing, not cursing. On and on they read. Ali knew that he could never come up to this standard. But as Samir explained the way of salvation Ali's heart began to soften.

After several hours the young men returned to the hotel. Ali continued to read whenever he had free time. Finally, one day he prayed out loud in his room, "Jesus, if You are real, make Yourself clear to me."

God met Ali in a most unusual way. He confessed his sins and became a child of God. His life was changed. Samir continued to disciple Ali with what he knew of God's Word.

During the days following the invasion of Lebanon by Israel, Ali returned to Lebanon. He wanted to tell his parents about his new faith in Christ. What a shock to find the area of the city where his parents lived completely devastated, his own home partially destroyed.

When Ali told his parents about his faith in Christ they were very displeased. They didn't threaten to kill him but they put him out of the house.

When Israel was forced to withdraw because of

world opinion, the PLO returned. Now Ali was in danger. He must not be recognized. He had to hide. He decided to live in the International Church building. He had stayed there before and he figured he would be safe there.

When fighting broke out again in the area where his parents lived, Ali mustered up his courage and asked his parents to come and live with him. By now the missionaries had been evacuated and he was alone in the three-story building. His parents surprised him by accepting his offer.

Ali's six brothers were still fighting with the PLO. One of his brothers told Ali that his name was on a hit list. He would have to move again. If he stayed he would certainly die at the hands of those who hated him.

Before Ali had time to leave that night, 25 armed men approached the building. What should he do? His heart was pounding. He could hardly breathe. There was nowhere to hide.

As he backed up against the wall, he remembered the story of Daniel in the lions' den.

"Oh, Lord Jesus," he prayed, "they are coming to kill me. You kept Daniel in the lions' den. Please keep me. Hide me from my enemies." He lifted up his arms toward heaven.

The men climbed the three flights of stairs, reached the apartment door, banged on it and shouted. Ali's mother, the only other one in the apartment, opened the door for them. Ali could hear the men shout, "Where is Ali?"

His mother answered, "Ali is not here."

"We'll find out if he is not here."

They began to search the apartment room by room. Finally, they came to his door. They opened the door and turned on the light. Ali was standing in full view with his back against the wall. The men looked around the room, but they did not see him.

Throwing Ali's mother on the floor, they shouted, "We'll get him yet," and they retreated down the stairs.

When Ali told us the story he added, "Either God blinded their eyes or He covered me with a cloud. They did not see me."

16

Land of Death and Danger

(Miriam)

L ebanon is a rather small country 130 miles long and 35 miles wide. It is a land of con-trasts—high mountains sometimes covered with snow paralleled by a rich fertile coastline bordering the Mediterranean Sea.

It is a strategic country commercially, educationally and financially, as well as being a pleasure center for the Middle East. Lebanon is the only non-Muslim country from Turkey south around the Mediterranean to the Atlantic Ocean.

There has been fighting for more than 15 years. People from outside the country continue to be involved in the conflict. There are differences of opinion on all sides. The following announcement appeared in a recent periodical: "If anyone thinks they know what the fighting in Lebanon is all about, they most certainly do not know what the fighting in Lebanon is all about."

During these many years of war, men, women

and children have been killed by the thousands. More than that, the occupants of the land have become killers. Young men in their 20s look to be 40.

In addition to the tremendous loss of life and property, a whole generation has lost hope. The children do not have a youth—they grow up overnight. They have seen everything good the future could hold crumble to the ground. They have been shot at by snipers. They have been killed in crossfire. Their homes have been shelled without notice and for no apparent reason. They are in constant danger of being detained, kidnapped or murdered.

Jaleel Safoury taught in an evangelical boys' school. He was known for his faithful witness for the Lord Jesus Christ.

He regularly attended our Wednesday evening prayer service if the situation allowed. He would freely tell of the many opportunities he had to witness for Christ. He would ask for prayer for the Muslim students at his school.

After prayer meeting he would often ask us to sit around the piano and sing. Many times we were very tired, but not wanting to disappoint him, we would stay and sing and sing and sing.

One Wednesday evening, during a particularly critical and uncertain time in the fighting, Jaleel did not come to the service. Thinking he was probably detained by his busy schedule, we did not worry.

Several days later we heard rumors that Jaleel was missing. No one knew why.

We soon found out that he been preparing refreshments for the blind students where he was living. In the midst of his work, someone came to say that a person at the gate wanted to talk with him.

Jaleel said, "Tell that person that I am busy now." The messenger came back reporting that the lady at the door insisted that Jaleel come—someone wanted to hear about Christ.

At the gate, Jaleel discovered that the woman was dressed in a typical Iranian headdress. She led Jaleel away from the house. He was never seen again.

After several days, Jaleel's sister became alarmed and began to inquire at some local hospitals and finally went to the morgue. With some persuasion, the attendant allowed her to inspect the numerous bodies that were as yet unclaimed.

Walking down row after row, she finally came to a decapitated corpse.

"That is my brother," she exclaimed.

The attendant was surprised.

"How do you know that is your brother?" he asked.

"I know this is my brother," she replied, "because of this birthmark on his hand. Furthermore, I made those colorful shorts for him with my very own hands."

Who killed Jaleel? Why did they kill him? Is there no revenge?

The first two questions have no answer at present. The last one does. Jesus said, "Vengeance is mine."

A Sunday Bomb

One Sunday afternoon Sami phoned to say that

his building had been bombed and their apartment was in ruins. We jumped in our car and sped over to Sami's place. Sure enough, there was a large gaping hole on the top floor. Unable to take the elevator, we picked our way carefully up the stairs through the debris.

We found Sami, his head covered with a towel, shoveling pieces of cement block and plaster out of their apartment. Thick layers of dust covered everything. The nauseating stench of death permeated the area. The Dagher family had missed a fatal blow by just minutes.

The owner of the apartment next door was a member of the private Lebanese militia. He made and stored bombs in his apartment. His wife and mother-in-law were in the apartment preparing refreshments for a celebration to be held later in the afternoon. While they were working the bomb exploded.

The Dagher family would have normally been home for lunch, very likely with guests. We were often included in their Sunday invitations. On this day, however, they had been delayed as they taxied members of their congregation to their homes after church.

Joy had arrived in the area first. She found the road to their apartment blocked by the police. She left the car and ran to the apartment.

Shortly afterward, Sami arrived. He was shocked to see a section of the top floor completely blown apart. Had his family been killed by the blast? He did not know.

As the story unfolded it was revealed that the explosion had scattered victims' bodies all over the neighborhood, even into the Daghers' apartment. Members of the neighboring family, who were downstairs at the time of the explosion, were in shock. People took sheets to gather up the fragmented flesh in the street, on the flat housetops and anywhere they could locate it.

The Daghers' efforts to restore their apartment were in vain. The only alternative was to move to the church in Karentina until they could locate a home elsewhere.

The Daghers lost many of their possessions in the blast, but they rejoiced that the God who preserves life also bountifully provides the needs of those who trust Him.

Beirut was a dangerous place. Fighting in the city would break out and no one seemed to know who started it or why. During lulls, everyone shopped for needed supplies. Some Sundays we were able to hold services, others we were not.

The whole populace was tense. The prudence of leaving home had to be weighed. There was always the possibility of remote control car bombings, flying barricades temporarily set up then suddenly relocated, check points with kidnappings, shelling and homes looted during the owners' absence.

Sharif-el-Akawi, a trusted radio announcer, often relayed helpful information. He would advise the safest streets to travel, giving the locations of any disturbances.

One day, after numerous cease-fires had broken down, Mr. Akawi yelled into the microphone: "There are armed snipers lurking everywhere. All

roads are unsafe. Blood maniacs are at large. I am
only human. I weep with my people. I feel your
desperation. We are losing Lebanon."

Preparing for a Crisis

In the light of the uncertain political situation, I
gave a devotional for the weekly women's meeting
on "Preparing for a Crisis." I realized that sooner or
later one or more of us in the group would face
such an experience. But I certainly could not have
predicted who it would be!

Psalm 34 was my text. I noted that David had
prepared for any eventuality by displaying an at-
titude of praise. He also accepted the circumstances that came into his life, knowing that they were
strained through the fire-screen of God's love, and
that nothing happens by chance to a child of God.

I assured the women that in any crisis we can cry
out to the Lord for refuge and safety. His power is
available to all who seek Him and are willing to obey
Him. Then I added, "Our knees may quake. We
may even shake all over in a crisis. We certainly may
not have the poise we want but we will have the
strength we need. We will not be paralyzed with fear
as God enables us to move through the crisis with
an inner confidence and a stabilizing peace. 'The
LORD is close to the brokenhearted . . . A righteous
man may have many troubles, but the LORD delivers
him from them all' (Psalm 34:18a, 19)."

The day after the women's meeting, Harry and I,
along with Sami, had planned to take Dr. Bob
Pierce to Beirut airport. Dr. Bob had come to minister in Lebanon even though he himself was dying
of leukemia. Except when preaching, he was in a

wheelchair most of the time.

Sami and Dr. Bob were waiting for us at the Bristol Hotel about five blocks from the International Church where we lived. The time to leave had come, but I had company in the living room. Harry noticed the guests and not wanting to be late, he quietly slipped out the side door and on up to the hotel. Soon the telephone rang.

"I'm at the Bristol," said Harry on the other end of the line. "I came on ahead. I didn't want to disturb you. There wasn't any shooting on the way. Do you mind walking up alone?"

"No, I'll be fine," I assured him. With the guests gone, I was heading out the door when the thought occurred to me: *Change your clothes. You want to look your best.*

I changed my clothes and was preparing to leave when the doorbell rang. I rushed to open it when another thought occurred to me: *It isn't wise to open the door without knowing who is on the other side.* Instead, I opened the little window in the door.

There stood a man, dressed in black. He thrust a gun through the grille of the window, aiming it directly at my head.

This is it, I thought momentarily. *This is my last moment on earth.* I tried to close the window, but the man broke it with his gun. The glass cut my arm. Although I was bleeding and shaking, my tongue was not paralyzed! I politely inquired in Arabic, "Shu betreed? (What is it you want?)"

I didn't wait for the answer but hurried into the dining room and shut and locked the door. Running to the edge of the balcony, I formed one hand into the shape of a gun and pointed to the stairwell with the other. "Help!" I shouted.

Neighbors stuck their heads out of the windows. Two men ran down the lane and brought back two of the No. 16 armed car unit police. They rushed up the three flights of stairs and I opened the door for them. They searched everywhere, but found no one. The intruder had evidently dashed down the staircase and over the back wall when I screamed.

I turned to the men.

"Thank you!" I said. "Now, will you please take me up to the Bristol Hotel? My husband is waiting for me to go to the airport."

Advising me that it was not their policy to transport people unless they are under arrest for some misdemeanor, they finally agreed to take me.

Arriving at the Bristol, I was greeted by Sami and Dr. Bob. Harry had left to try to find me. He had expected me over an hour earlier and became alarmed when I did not arrive.

"What happened to you?" Dr. Bob asked noticing the bloodstained dish towel wrapped around my arm. As I told them my story, he put his hands on my shoulders, and though the lobby was filled with people, he lifted his face toward heaven and thanked God out loud for my deliverance.

Harry returned and we left for the airport.

My message at the women's meeting? It was for me!

17

Friends

(Miriam)

Natasha and Nuira

At our International Church in Beirut one Sunday morning a flaxen-haired young woman walked down the aisle. We had never seen her before. I noticed that she listened to the message very attentively.

After the service we discovered her name was Natasha Rihani. She said her mother was Russian, her father Jordanian. They were divorced and she was now living with her father and stepmother.

A few weeks later we visited the Rihani apartment. We could readily see that Natasha was unhappy and that she did not feel comfortable there. After we had been talking for a while, her father, in obvious exasperation, said, "I don't know what to do with Natasha. She's a problem."

Without any hesitation I blurted, "Let us have her. We'll take her."

"Go ahead and take her," the father said with a sigh of relief. And so we headed home with a newly adopted daughter. It seemed a good idea at the time, but we had no idea what we were in for!

First of all, Natasha didn't like to be disciplined. One day we took her to visit her father. Her disrespectful behavior troubled me. Her father had been obviously disturbed by her actions as well. I was sure he must have been disappointed to see such little improvement in his daughter.

Natasha and I talked at length. Although I sympathized with her personal hurts, I told her that her father had been deeply hurt by her bitter words. I also told her we loved her and that I was sure there would be some solution.

And then, for a reason I cannot explain, I went up to her and took her by the shoulders. Looking her in the eyes, I said, "Natasha, whatever is in you is going to come out."

I was surprised to hear myself say such a thing. But, all of a sudden, her eyes went glassy and she fell to the floor in a heap. I ran to Harry.

"I think we have a very deep-seated problem to deal with," I blurted.

"It's time for prayer meeting," Harry said. "Let's ask the Lord for wisdom."

Usually Natasha would sit on a chair and participate in the meeting. This time, however, she sat on the floor by my chair and held onto my hand as though she were afraid I would leave her.

After we had said goodbye to everyone we went back up to Harry's study to talk and pray with Natasha. Harry read from the Scripture about Jesus and His dealings with evil spirits. Then he prayed.

I kept my eyes open. I couldn't believe what I saw! Natasha's eyes were glassy. Her body struggled.

The process of casting out the evil spirits lasted several weeks, but finally the day came when Natasha was able to give us her real name and not the name of a demon when asked.

One day as we were talking, she told me that her mother needed help. She was living alone and was fearful because of the war. We had met her mother previously and had visited her during heavy fighting in the city.

Nuira was crying when we arrived at her home. In fact, she was so distraught that we invited her to come and live temporarily with us, an offer she readily accepted.

Each day Nuira went to work at a stylish dress shop. At home, she would often sit down at the piano and play like a professional. She carried herself with an elegant air and was obviously accustomed to fine things and an expensive lifestyle. As the days wore on our relationship deepened.

One day Nuira and I were drinking coffee together.

"Nuira," I said, "you are Russian. I have had several other friends in my life who also were Russian."

I continued. "The first friend I ever really loved," I said, "was a Russian girl in Jerusalem when I was a girl. Mother and I led her to know Jesus Christ, but after we went home to the States on furlough, I received a letter telling me she had died of a broken neck when she fell off a donkey."

At that, Nuira's eyes filled with tears and she started to sob. What had I said to cause such a reaction?

She looked at me quizically.

"Was her name Valentina Kolikova?" she asked.

"Yes," I replied, surprised. "How did you know?"

"Valentina was my sister. I was a little girl when she fell off the donkey. You say she accepted Jesus Christ as her Savior? She must have prayed for our family. There were pictures of Valentina all over our house. My parents mourned her death till they died. That was 50 years ago. You have traveled around the world many times and I have traveled, too. And now here we are in Beirut, together, in the midst of an awful war. It is dangerous here, yet we are both still alive. This is no accident. God has brought us together. It is an answer to prayer."

(Harry)

Barry

One Sunday during the morning service at the church I was midway through my message when my attention was drawn to the entrance of the sanctuary.

Beyond the veranda I saw someone peering through the upright railing. I could see that he was crying.

A woman sitting in the back pew of the chapel also saw the visitor. She rushed out to investigate and they both disappeared from my view. As soon as the benediction was pronounced, the woman came in to tell me that a very troubled young man was waiting outside to see me.

With difficulty, because of his intoxication, I ushered him to a seat in the front of the chapel. He kept mumbling, "They almost killed me. They almost killed me."

Through his sobs we learned that he worked as an oil driller down in Saudi Arabia. The workers were permitted two weeks out of each month to come to Beirut for R & R.

While in Beirut, he often visited the strip. Early that Sunday morning, after a night of drinking, he had gotten into a fight with someone at the bar. He groaned as he told me how his opponent had pinned him to the floor and attempted to kill him. Somehow he had gotten loose and had staggered to the street where he hailed a taxi and told the driver to take him to church. Of all the churches in Beirut, the taxi brought him to ours.

During the conversation it suddenly occurred to me (I believe the Holy Spirit brought it to my mind) that we had received a letter from a lady in Canada asking us to look out for her son who worked in Saudi Arabia and visited Beirut occasionally. Could this be her son?

"What's your name?" I asked.

"Davey Crockett!" he responded.

Surely he was kidding!

I ventured, "I received a letter from your mother."

"Oh, yes, my mother," he slurred.

Suddenly I remembered the name of the young man mentioned in the letter.

"Barry," I said, "your mother asked us to pray for

you and to watch out for you and here you are."

This young man had been brought up in a Christian home but had strayed far from his moorings. In answer to his mother's faithful prayers, the Lord had followed him even to Lebanon.

The people of the church took Barry under their wing and nurtured him. He became involved in Bible studies in Saudi Arabia and later married a Christian girl. Just recently we received word from his mother praising the Lord for so miraculously answering prayer for her son.

(Harry)

Zadan

To celebrate special occasions in Beirut we often went with a group to the Bristol Hotel to dine. After dinner Sami would ask the waiter to invite Zadan, the hotel's chef, to come out to talk to us. Zadan and Sami had worked together.

Zadan had accumulated considerable wealth which included 25 apartments. Sami had witnessed to Zadan many times. He was always polite and even friendly, but that was as far as he was willing to go.

In the winter of 1983, the 25 apartments Zadan owned were leveled to the ground in city fighting. Overnight Zadan went from riches to rags.

After this great loss, Sami received a phone call. He found Zadan and his wife, Jamal, and three sons living with nine other families in a bombed-out basement with water covering the floor. Now Zadan was ready to hear God's Word.

Sami opened his Bible and began to read. Right

there, in a flooded, bombed-out basement, Zadan
and his entire family accepted Christ and became a
great blessing in the Karentina church.

(Harry)

Hudha and May

Hudha was a charming young high school girl
who attended the International Church. She loved
the Lord and had a deep desire to serve Him.

Hudha had made friends with a Muslim girl
named May. May's parents liked Hudha and appreciated her outgoing personality, her high stand-
ards and her friendliness.

As time went on, May accepted Christ through
Hudha's testimony. Then the girls began to work
on a plan to get May to church. Finally, they came
up with the idea that May could ask for permission
to visit Hudha on Sunday morning. The girls would
then take the phone off the hook and go to church.
Thus her family couldn't inquire about her and
May would be back home before they would become suspicious. The plan worked.

The high school where the girls attended was not
far from the church. Often they would come down
at noon to eat their lunches, sing and play the
piano. One day, they appeared at my office door.

"We want to be baptized and we would like to be
baptized at the same time."

This didn't surprise me, but I knew it would be
very unwise to baptize a Muslim girl before she was
of age. I explained the problem and they decided
to wait until after May's birthday.

Some months later the girls appeared again at my

door. They were so excited. They informed me that May was now of age and asked when the next baptismal service would be held. Inasmuch as there was no baptistry in the church we usually held the service elsewhere—in another church or at a public beach on the Mediterranean.

The day finally arrived. It was a beautiful Sunday afternoon. Everything had been arranged, even to a platform on the beach for the candidates to use when they gave their testimonies. The multi-national members of our church stood around with their hymnbooks in hand.

I sighted Hudha and May coming down the beach toward us and walked over to greet them.

"Where are the baptismal robes?" Hudha asked.

"Oh," I said, "last Sunday I announced that the robes had been misplaced during our recent move and that the candidates would have to make their own arrangements."

The girls had not heard the announcement. Now what were they going to do?

"I have permission to be out only until five o'clock," May exclaimed. "I certainly can't go home soaking wet. What would I tell my parents?"

The only solution I had to offer was that the girls wait until the next baptismal service.

We began the service and proceeded with the testimonies and singing. Suddenly I felt a tug on my shirtsleeve. There stood Hudha and May. They were all smiles.

"Mr. Taylor," they said, "we have found a way to get baptized."

I told them to stand up on the platform and give

their testimonies. By this time the crowd of on-lookers had increased considerably with many beach roamers mixing in with the congregation. The girls gave a clear witness of what the Lord Jesus meant in their lives.

After the preliminaries, they went off to a nearby tent where May put on Hudha's clothes and Hudha put on May's clothes. May came down to the beach and was one of the first to be baptized. Her joy could not be hidden—she was radiant!

Then the girls returned to the tent. Hudha put on her own wet clothes that May had worn to be bap-tized and May put on her dry clothes. Then they both came back down to the beach and Hudha was baptized, the last in line. What ingenuity!

May's parents began bringing young Muslim men to the house, asking May to choose which one she would like to marry.

May, however, told her parents that there was something wrong with every one of them—they are all blind. Of course, she meant spiritually blind.

Then came a very dark day. May's parents found her Bible, her hymnbook and some Christian litera-ture. More serious yet, they discovered that she had been baptized a Christian.

In the Muslim culture, uncles have a strong in-fluence on the whole family. One day, an uncle brought a sheikh to the house in order to argue Christianity out of May. Holding the Koran in his hand, the sheikh began his lecture. When he stopped to take a breath, May interrupted.

"Tell me," she said, "when a person knows he has sin in his heart and life and realizes he is under the judgment of God, is there anything in that book to help the sinner?"

The sheikh slammed the Koran shut and glaring at May said, "Young lady, I have no answers for you." He put his Koran under his arm and stomped out of the house.

May's uncle was furious. He jumped to his feet and screamed to his brother, May's father, "Throw this girl out in the street."

May turned to her father and said, "Father, someone has to go. Will it be Uncle or me?"

To everyone's amazement, May's father turned to her and said, "May, you have the truth." He then put his brother out of the house.

Because of the war we have not seen May since that time, but we have learned that she was finally forced to marry a Muslim. He permits her to read her Bible and they sometimes read it together.

18

The Luncheons

(Miriam)

It was Christmas 1968 and a dream of mine was about to come true. Our first women's luncheon, sponsored by the International Church, was to be a part of our Christmas celebration.

It was decided that the luncheon would be held in our home. The speaker would be Lucy Dagelman Sullivan, a classmate from Nyack days and now a professor at the Beirut College for Women.

The luncheon was a smashing success with 25 women in attendance. The following year, 71 women attended. Another miracle.

The third luncheon precipitated a relationship that lasts to this day.

The speaker at the luncheon had been Hazel St. John, the principal of the Evangelical Girls' School in West Beirut. She had previously been decorated with a medal by the president of Lebanon for her contribution to the education of its young people. She had also been decorated by the queen of England for her contribution to education in Arab lands. Hazel was an elegant Christian woman, always friendly and self-sacrificing.

She gave a brief devotional and then introduced one of the teachers from her school who spoke in Arabic as Hazel interpreted it into English.

The teacher had lived in Damour, a Christian village on the road that led from Beirut to Sidon. Terrorists had repeatedly threatened her village. Some of the people had fled, fearing what the future might hold. Others, still undecided, remained.

One night, the insurgents forced their way into the village, shooting to the right and to the left. Those who tried to flee were captured, tortured, mistreated, mutilated. Young girls especially were abused and then killed. When the rebels had spent their rage on the population, they began to loot and burn. The village was totally destroyed. The speaker and her family had escaped without bodily injury, but their minds and hearts bore the scars of that experience.

It was in the aftermath of this stirring presentation that I met Lydia. She seemed very anxious to talk, to unload her burdened heart. With so many women crowding around, she asked to see me.

"Be prepared to weep with me," she said. "I have a sad story to tell you."

A few days later I walked the short distance to Lydia's apartment. She had prepared tea and refreshments. I love Middle East hospitality—visitors are really honored and made to feel welcome.

We went into the living room and began to talk. She told me that her husband, Ali, worked in Saudi Arabia and that they had three children, all at

school. Hardly stopping for a breath, Lydia poured
out her story.

Her Russian parents had immigrated to Argen-
tina where Lydia grew up speaking both Russian
and Spanish. One day an aunt from Boston came
to visit. At her aunt's invitation, Lydia went to Boston with her. She completed her high school education and studied at Gordon College. In her second
year there, she had to drop out because of surgery.
After recuperating, she went to Moody Bible Institute because she felt God calling her to be a missionary.

After graduation she was sent by a small missionary organization to teach in a Bible school in Ar-
gentina. But after only one year the society notified
Lydia that they could no longer finance her ministry. She returned to the States.

Then she met Ali, a Lebanese studying to be an
engineer. He was tall and handsome and spoke
English very well. He agreed to go to the church
Lydia attended and professed to be a Christian.

Soon they were married but Lydia realized almost immediately that she had made a serious mistake. Ali had not had a change of heart. He was
not a true believer in Christ.

Lydia tried to pray, but her prayers seemed to go
no higher than the ceiling. She tried to read her
Bible but it did not speak to her heart. All was
dark. She was afraid.

Their son, Hussein, was born and the family
moved to Saudi Arabia where Ali was to be
employed.

Two more children were born there—Sami and

Nadia. As they grew older Lydia eventually had to move to Lebanon for their education. Ali had rented the apartment where they were now living. Sami, the second-born child, had just been diagnosed with leukemia.

"I know that I have sinned against God," Lydia cried. "I have disobeyed the Scripture that says believers are not to marry unbelievers. I need to confess my sin and ask God to forgive me. I have been so unhappy."

We prayed and there was confession with many tears. Peace came to Lydia's heart. I left Lydia's home just as the children—Hussein, Sami and Nadia—returned from school.

Before long, all three children had accepted Jesus, too. When Ali discovered this, he was furious and demanded that the children start to study with a Muslim sheikh so as to change their minds. However, Ali soon saw that that was useless and the lessons were discontinued.

Little Sami's leukemia became worse and he finally had to be hospitalized. When Harry heard that Sami was dying he hurried to the hospital. As he was reading the 23rd Psalm, Ali walked in. Though he didn't participate in the prayer, he didn't hinder either.

Ali then went out on the porch. Harry followed him. Silently they stood together for some moments. Then Harry said, "Ali, little Sami is dying. He is a Christian and will soon be going to heaven. If you ever hope to see him again, you will have to become a believer, too."

Ali turned to Harry and said, "Mr. Taylor, leave

me alone. I am a Muslim and I will never change."
"If that is the way you want it," Harry said, "that's
the way it will be."
Not long after, little Sami went to be with Jesus.
Ali took the body to his village in the Bekkha Valley
to give him a Muslim burial. Lydia did not go. Her
heart was broken. She couldn't even give Sami a
Christian burial.

Due to the heavy fighting in Beirut, Lydia and
the two children returned to Saudi Arabia. But
Ali's resentment became explosive and he finally
bought Lydia and the children tickets to return to
the States. He said he could not live under the
same roof with Christians.

With the passage of the years of war in Lebanon,
many of the women who attended the luncheons
are now scattered around the world. Only eternity
will reveal their heart responses to the presentation
of God's Word and the testimonies of His interven-
tion in people's lives.

19

The Miracle of the Shoulder Bags

(Miriam)

I t was the afternoon before Christmas in Beirut. Many plans had been formulated, all of which were dependent on the political situation of the moment. The Daghers had invited us to their home on the east side of the city. We would also celebrate my birthday and open our gifts Christmas Eve in order to be ready to get up early Christmas morning to attend the services at the Karentina Church.

In preparing to cross over into East Beirut, we were forced, as always, to consider all available information on the situation at the Green Line. At that time the Green Line's museum crossing was the only open connection in the divided city. On both sides, barricades of sand bags and walls of shipping containers reinforced the imaginary, but nevertheless real, line of demarcation.

Between the barricades lay no man's land which was by no means safe. Snipers often telescoped their victims from the rooftops and walls of destroyed buildings. Filled with apprehension, we prayed for wisdom.

Although I was feeling somewhat weak after an attack of the flu, we packed our bags and wrapped the gifts for the Dagher family. Our most valuable and important personal items were placed, as usual, in two shoulder bags. We always carried these bags with us if we were leaving home for even a short time.

Harry carried the two suitcases and the two shoulder bags from our third-floor apartment down the three flights of stairs. Outside our gate we met our neighbor. "I am hesitant to go out to the airport to work today," he said. "I hear there is shooting out that way."

We also had to go in that direction to get to the museum crossing. We were uneasy. Should we attempt it? Several cars were lined up in the lane behind us, blocking access to Abul Aziz Street. Shoppers always found it convenient to park in our lane. We got in the car and backed it up over the curb and down the sidewalk. Finally at the street, traffic was extremely heavy. If so many others could travel on this troubled day, we thought, so could we.

We arrived at the crossing without incident. We had passed the road that led to the airport, and yes, there had been some checkpoints along the way, but the guards hadn't detained us for long.

Now for the dash across no man's land. Harry pushed the accelerator to the floor. What a relief it was to arrive safely at the other side. We thanked the Lord. Once more we had made it safely.

We drove on up the mountain to the Daghers' home without incident. The whole family came out to welcome us and help carry our bags to our room.

After a delicious birthday meal, we went into the living room to open our gifts. I was especially pleased with a beautiful wool skirt from Joy and I wanted to put it on. I slipped out of the room and headed to the bedroom to change. I had packed an extra blouse in my shoulder bag. The shoulder bag! No shoulder bag was in sight!

Running back to the living room, I exclaimed, "Harry, did you bring everything in from the car?"

"I thought I did," he answered.

Sami and Harry rushed out to the car to look. My heart sank as I saw them return empty handed. All our valuables were in those two bags. I had failed to count the bags before we left home. How could I have forgotten? I was always counting bags! Fortunately, this time I had put our passports and identity cards in my purse. At least they were safely in our possession.

"Mr. Taylor," announced Sami, "we are going to go over to your apartment and look for your bags."

It was already dark and not safe to drive anywhere. Usually the shooting increased at night and there were always checkpoints. But Sami was determined.

How silly, I thought to myself. *Those shoulder bags certainly aren't worth risking two lives!*

After Harry and Sami had left, Joy and Paul and Anna (the Daghers' two children) and I sat down to talk and pray. My heart was heavy.

As we talked and prayed, I gradually began to relax and relinquished the contents of the bags to the Lord. It would be all right, I decided, if I never saw them again.

We waited and we waited. We knew it would take a long time to go over to West Beirut and back, but it was now past nine o'clock. Could something have happened to the men? What was keeping them all this time?

Finally, we heard a car. The doorbell rang, not a casual ring, but an insistent one.

We opened the door and there stood Sami and Harry, the shoulder bags over their arms!

The men reported that they had been turned back from several streets because of fighting, but that they had found some open streets and finally pulled safely into the lane leading to the church.

Here they bumped into "Mamma," the lady of the "mystery house" next door. As refugees from the south, Mamma and her family had occupied this condemned house some months before. We guessed that the young men of the family were fighters for they would be gone for days at a time.

Mamma seemed to be the boss. Whenever anyone needed money, she would reach into her bra and dole it out. Once she managed to steal 13 watermelons behind the back of a vendor while he was weighing and selling only one to Harry!

"Have you seen two shoulder bags?" Sami asked Mamma.

"Yes! I saw those bags. They are right inside the iron gate beside the church door." *How was it she*

had seen them but had not stolen them? Harry
wondered.

Acting as a guide, Mamma led the way, relating
what had happened that afternoon.

"After you left," she said, "a woman wearing a
gold necklace was walking down Abdul Aziz Street.
A man came up from behind and grabbed her
necklace. He darted up the lane, through the open
iron gate and up the stairs to the top floor.
Another man, seeing the incident, pursued the
thief, shooting into the air all the way. I went to see
what was going on. That is when I noticed the two
shoulder bags. There they are."

Unbelievable! A robber, a fleeing gunman and
Mamma had all had access to those bags, but not
one had touched them!

It was time for our furlough. We had asked for
someone to replace us. Could anyone be found to
come to this violent city? The days were so uncertain. Would they be safe?

The Russell Clarks, our replacements, arrived just
two days before our scheduled departure.

And yes, God would take care of them just as He
had miraculously taken care of the two shoulder
bags!

Part V

Syria: A Kernel of Wheat—Much Fruit

God at first showed his concern by taking from the Gentiles a people for himself. (Acts 15:14)

20

On Their Own

(Harry)

In the early years, The Christian and Missionary Alliance work spread from Palestine to Trans-Jordan and then on to Syria. The Alliance had been asked by a small Mission to take over their work in Syria, particularly the Christian schools that had been started.

Syria, at that time, was one of the least evangelized fields in Muslim areas that were open to the gospel. Today, about 10 percent of Syria is Christian, that is to say, non-Muslim. Of this percentage, the greater portion is nominal. The largest, Bible-centered, evangelical denomination in Syria is The Christian and Missionary Alliance.

When the State of Israel was decreed by the United Nations in 1948, the Syrian government looked with suspicion on all evangelical, foreign missionaries, especially Americans. The U.S. government favored the existence of the State of Israel, they said.

In 1960 the last missionaries were expelled from

Syria, but Syrian believers were permitted to continue services under strict and constant government observation.

When we took the assignment to the Near East in 1966 we were allowed to drive through Syria to get to Jordan. We did not visit in Syria except on rare occasions with special permission obtained from the government by the pastors. Church services were under close surveillance by the secret police.

Once a year, however, the churches of Lebanon, Syria and Jordan got together for their annual six-day conference in Lebanon where complete freedom was enjoyed. This fellowship of the believers was a highlight of the year, an uplifting celebration for everyone.

The believers from the Syrian churches seemed unusually committed to the Lord in spite of laboring under severe restrictions and suspicion.

Rev. Ibrahim Oueis

In 1948 Rev. Ibrahim Oueis went to Syria from Palestine where he had been pastoring a church in Jerusalem. Many of the Arab believers evacuated to Syria with him. A stable congregation was formed, but there was no consistent financial support for Pastor Oueis.

The church services, held in a rented apartment, were often disturbed by the neighbors. The apartment also limited the group's growth potential.

In 1965, when the Breadens were about to retire, a self-support program in which the Mission would no longer release funds to support national pastors was put into effect. Many wondered how Ibrahim

Oueis and the other pastors in Syria would accept the news.

As was his practice, Ibrahim came to Beirut for his monthly visit and to get his remittance. Dad Breaden had the difficult task of informing him about the new policy: each pastor was to be cut 25 percent a year for four years.

At first, the news surprised Ibrahim. But after a few moments he announced, "I'll take my cuts all at once. Now."

This decision on the part of Pastor Oueis called for a giant step of faith! His own congregation would now be expected to support him and his family of four children—Paul, Louise, John and Philip. The former policy had provided foreign funds to finance every aspect of the work. (This practice was prevalent throughout the Middle East in other Missions as well.)

Pastor Oueis returned to Damascus, praying all the way. "Lord, I am facing a difficult problem. I need wisdom. Give me a message out of Your Word to give my people. May they understand the biblical concept of tithing."

On Sunday he preached from Second Kings 3:17: "You will see neither wind nor rain, yet this valley will be filled with water." He challenged his people to start making their trenches and digging their ditches. He encouraged them to do all that was in their power and strength to do according to the will of the Lord. God would do the rest.

He closed his message with the words, "There may be no visible facts to stand on. Even though there be no cloud, wind or rain, there will be water.

God is the God of miracles!"

One man, a jeweler, stood to his feet and announced he was going to start tithing immediately.
Others followed his example. The owner of the Al
Raja Hotel also felt the conviction of the Holy
Spirit. We usually stayed at his hotel when visiting
in Damascus. He would phone the pastor when we
arrived and say, "Miriam is here." (My name is a
typical Arabic name—Meriam.) If the pastor
thought it was safe for us to visit the parsonage, he
would say, "Ahlan wa sahlan (welcome)." This
would give us the liberty to visit.

There was a definite reason why we all had to be
cautious. For two years Pastor Oueis had been
under surveillance. At times, he had even been
under house arrest. When he was found to be innocent of all suspicion and the false charges that
had been leveled against him, the government gave
him considerable freedom to travel about, to
receive guests and to minister.

After this period, he was appointed by the Syrian
government to be the official representative of the
Protestant faith to interview Protestant women
who came to Syria with the intention of marrying
Muslim men. The law required that any Christian
who desired to marry a Muslim had to renounce
his or her former Christian faith and accept Islam
at the marriage ceremony. Ibrahim used the interview as an opportunity to share the gospel.

In the midst of all of this change, Pastor Oueis
had a vision to purchase land and build a church.
Their present meeting room was in the center of a
Muslim sector and the commotion in the surround-

ing apartments continued to increase until it became almost impossible for the preacher to be heard by the congregation.

The situation pushed Ibrahim to begin searching for a suitable piece of property for the proposed building. One day he went for a long walk and found what he wanted. He told Antoinette, his wife, that he had found just the right place.

"Our people have just begun to support us," she exclaimed. "Now, so quickly, you want them to take on a heavier burden?"

"The Lord will provide," Ibrahim answered with conviction.

When the members of the congregation heard about the prospect of building their own facility, they agreed to start a fund. The Breadens also made the project known through their prayer letters. It was amazing how God worked! Even students at the Indonesian Bible School heard about the anticipated church and sent a contribution.

By the time we arrived in the Near East, in 1966, the building project was well on its way. On our infrequent trips to Syria, Ibrahim took great delight in showing us what had been accomplished since our last visit. Little by little the church began to take shape. The auditorium seated about 500 people, with additional seating in the balcony. A large lighted sign on the roof proclaimed, "Jesus, the Light of the World."

Ibrahim worked very hard, preaching near and far, sometimes two or three times a day. His heart could not take the strain and he was soon confined to bed. We came home on furlough and before long heard that he had gone to be with the Lord whom He loved and served with his whole heart. His very capable son-in-law, Fareed Khoury, succeeded him as pastor and also as president of The Christian and Missionary Alliance in Syria.

At the centennial celebration in March, 1990, in Amman, Jordan, it was reported that 16 new works had been opened in Syria. Praise the Lord!

Operation Hitchhiker

Picking up hitchhikers is not a recommended practice in any country, but Sami Dagher picks up hitchhikers wherever he goes, even at midnight!

On one trip Sami picked up a Syrian truck driver and then, a little further down the road, two Lebanese soldiers. Sensing the soldiers' hate for the Syrian, Sami pushed the truck driver out of the car at the next check point.

But Sami was totally unprepared for what happened next—the soldiers' anger became redirected at him to the point of ordering him to drive to a secluded area. They seemed intent on killing Sami.

Sami refused to go and eventually was able to placate the soldiers.

Did such a close call end Operation Hitchhiker? No, not at all.

Some time later, Sami picked up another soldier on that same mountain road. This man turned out to be a Syrian officer, so Sami invited him home for lunch. Surprisingly, the officer accepted.

On the way home, Sami stopped to buy some roasted chicken. He also telephoned Joy to tell her to put on her best table service for he was bringing a Syrian Muslim officer to eat with them.

"You Syrian soldiers," Sami said, "are our enemy and if something hadn't happened in my heart, I would be killing you instead of feeding you." He went on to tell how Jesus Christ had changed his life.

The officer gave no indication that he was interested in what he was hearing. After they had eaten, Sami took the officer on to his destination. It had been a disappointing encounter.

Operation Hitchhiker II—The Sequel

The Alliance church in Damascus, Syria, was carrying on an aggressive witness to university students. Everyone knew that the church had been investigated several times by the government secret police because of their success in the student ministry among both Christians and Muslims.

In Syria, the government pays for the education of students. They are then obligated to serve the government for a specified length of time.

A young dental graduate had been led to Christ and was sent out to practice under a government-sponsored program. He was told to set up his clinic in a completely Muslim area far away from any Christian center. He complied with the order but he placed Bibles on the waiting room table and it wasn't long before Bible studies had started in homes and people were accepting Christ.

The Muslim Brotherhood heard about this and was furious. The Muslim religion doesn't dialogue with their opponents who threaten them—they just wipe them out. Some wanted to kill the dentist, but cooler heads prevailed.

"No, the dentist is working for the government.

If we kill him outright, we can only guess what will happen to us."

Another said, "Yes, we might be killed, too. There is no profit in doing that. I think there is a better way. There is more than one way to poison a person." (In Syria, a person is guilty until he can prove himself innocent.)

They decided to report the dentist to the government in Damascus. Why not let the government take the responsibility of disposing of him? They assembled all the accusations they could think of and a delegation went to Damascus to make the presentation.

Soon a Syrian official arrived at the dentist's office to investigate the accusations. The official went through the long list of complaints. Then, out of the blue, he asked, "Do you know Sami Dagher?"

The dentist thought a moment. *How could this Syrian know Sami, a Lebanese? What has Sami done? What could the Syrian government be doing with Sami?* he wondered. Despite the swirl of questions going through his mind he knew he had to tell the truth.

"Yes. I know Sami Dagher."

"Do you believe like Sami Dagher believes?"

Without hesitation, the dentist answered, "Yes, I do believe like Sami believes."

"If you believe like Sami does, you keep right on doing what you are doing. If you have any more trouble with these people, just let me know. I will come back and take care of them."

Who was that official? He was the Syrian officer Sami had picked up on the mountain road in Lebanon and later fed at his table.

Part VI

Jordan: An Open Door

That the remnant of men may seek the Lord,
and all the Gentiles who bear my name. (Acts 15:17)

21

With the Sun and the Sea

(Miriam)

Jordan is unique in that the Christian faith has been tolerated more there than in any other Muslim country in the Near East. About 20 percent of the population is Christian. As in Syria, the majority of those are nominal Christians.

Missionaries have been generally accepted. This openness to Christianity is largely due to King Hussein's concept of democratic freedom and his willingness to stand up to the ancient bias of past religious tradition. The king sees the Christian presence as a positive contribution to his country, not only in the sphere of religion but also in economics and education.

The Albert Hashweh Family

It was in Beersheba in September, 1923, that I first met Albert Hashweh. Our five-member Breaden family had arrived to take up residence on the Beersheba Mission compound. At that time,

Beersheba was a rather small town on the edge of the desert. A British military installation was situated on the other side of the marketplace, quite a distance from us. Other buildings included the railroad station, the Mission compound, some houses with flat roofs and a Muslim mosque.

Besides the railroad trains, the only motorized means of conveyance were military vehicles and our own motorcycle with a sidecar. Otherwise there were only camels and donkeys. I will always remember the many wells in the area. The name Beersheba means "seven wells."

The Mission house graced the front of a large walled-in compound. At the rear of the property was a church building complete with belfry, a school and rooms for the teachers. Albert Hashweh attended this school. Albert's parents prayed that their son would some day serve the Lord. Though there were many circumstances and events that could have hindered Albert—such as a military career—God was faithful and Albert became a dedicated Christian leader.

Albert and his wife raised seven children under very difficult circumstances, but their faith in God sustained them. All seven of their children married and continue to follow the Lord. This dedicated family formed the foundation for enlarged and productive outreach of the gospel in Jordan and throughout the Middle East.

At first, Albert was forced to take secular work to help support his family. The believers were giving their tithes and offerings, but it wasn't enough. For many years all meetings were held in a section of the Hashweh home. The room seated only 50, but sometimes for special occasions they managed to squeeze in double that number by using the bedrooms on either side. People sat on the beds, in the doorways and around the platform.

Albert Hashweh was elected president of the Alliance in Jordan in 1956. For 33 years he sacrificed and sustained a clear testimony. He sought to win souls for Christ and establish them into the local church.

Before Albert went to be with the Lord in 1989, he was able to attend the ground-breaking ceremony for the new Second Circle Alliance Church. At the dedication of the church in 1990, Albert's son, Yousef, a graduate of Alliance Theological Seminary, was ordained and took his father's place as pastor. He was also elected president of the National Church.

Manhal Zuraicat, the Architect

Manhal was won to Christ by Victor Hashweh, one of Albert's sons. Victor and Manhal were high school students when Victor invited Manhal, a Greek Orthodox, to attend his church.

Soon Manhal accepted Christ and became very enthusiastic about his faith. During the years he studied architecture at the Arab University in Beirut, he attended our church, and before long began leading Arabic language services.

While in Beirut, he fell in love with Hudha, the girl who was baptized in the wet clothes! After Manhal received his degree, their marriage was announced.

On the day before the wedding the fighting was

particularly severe and travel was dangerous. But, no matter, fighting or not, the wedding took place as planned.

Harry had been asked to escort the bride down the aisle in a little improvised living room-turned-chapel at the home of a relative. It was a beautiful wedding. The city was quiet for most of the day.

The Zuraicats went to live in Jordan where Manhal worked as an architect. He eventually attended Fuller Theological Seminary and returned to Jordan to launch and to pastor the Sixth Circle Church in Amman.

The Telegram

When I think of Jordan an experience comes to my mind which was one of the most painful yet victorious of my Christian life.

It was May 12th and we were in Madaba, Jordan, for the Sunday services. The day was almost over when a friend came into the church just before the evening service.

"Miriam," he said, "you received a phone call from the States this afternoon at the Hashweh home and they phoned us here just a few minutes ago. They will call again tomorrow morning. Be in Amman by 10 o'clock." There was no mention of who had called and, although I was curious, I felt no apprehension.

By 10 o'clock Monday morning I was sitting by the phone at the Hashweh's home.

The telephone rang.

"Mother, we're leaving for the funeral right now. I wanted so much to talk to you yesterday." It was Judy's voice on the phone.

"Whose funeral?" I asked.

"Grandma Breaden's funeral. Didn't you know?"

I was devastated! The last I had heard my mother was improving and was able to sit up to eat her meals. A sudden stroke took her. She was gone!

The telegram arrived later that day.

It seemed that my heart had been torn in pieces for about two years for one reason or another. Blow after blow! Conflict after conflict! Wars from without and heart struggles within. I thought it would never end!

My journal expressed it best:

> The most recent struggle is to have my mother taken just two months before we are to go home on furlough. I have tried over and over again to commit it all to the Lord. But no peace!
>
> Last week I received a letter from a friend. This is what she said: "You could, no doubt, be mad at God for being in such a hurry to take your mother home to heaven." This shocked me. I would never want to think that. Then I began to analyze my feelings and reactions. I discovered that even though I was trying, in my own strength, to be victorious, I wasn't really succeeding. If I can't say, "Praise the Lord, she was taken away from her suffering," I was bordering on blaming God for not knowing what He was doing. So maybe I am mad at God underneath, even though I don't realize it. I don't want to do that.

I searched my heart. Was I harboring unforgiveness toward others? Was I refusing to submit the situations of my life into His care? Was I fretting over things I could not change anyway? I confessed everything that was bothering me and I asked God for forgiveness. It is hard to explain, but peace flooded my soul—a wonderful peace that only a gentle, loving, forgiving Heavenly Father can supply. Yes, there was pain, but there was also peace—and victory.

(Harry)

Mr. T, the Iraqi
(Many details of this story have been changed or omitted to protect the persons involved.)

In Amman, Jordan, the Lord gave us the unique experience of making friends and enjoying fellowship with Mr. T, a most remarkable person. A former Iraqi general, he was a well-educated Muslim with many natural talents.

After the king of Iraq was overthrown, the military leaders, including Mr. T, and others faithful to the king were rounded up and thrown into jail. The cells were packed so full that the men could only stand upright, kept hours at a time without relief. He did not see the sun for seven months. He was beaten until his clothes were soaked with blood. He was hung up by his hands and made to stand on his tiptoes. He tried to fight off sleep, knowing that if he relaxed, his arms would be pulled out of joint. It happened. Unable to use his arms, He was forced to eat his food like a dog, from a plate on the floor.

The rebels began to execute the jailed leaders one by one. Day after day, he heard the victims led out to face the firing squad. He cried out to the God of heaven, "Oh, God, don't let them kill me."

As the days passed, the arm of the executioner kept coming closer to his cell. Finally, the day came when he knew he was next. That day, however, the soldiers passed by his cell and took the man just past him. The Lord had spared his life.

The next turn of events seemed to be a twist of fate. The rebel government suddenly discovered they had killed the most capable of the country's military leaders, so Mr. T was taken out of solitary confinement and reassigned. Due to his great capabilities and popularity, however, Mr. T was once again dismissed and thrown back into jail.

In a unique turn of circumstances, Mr. T was spirited out of the country dressed as a woman and eventually arrived in Amman, Jordan, where we met him. Each time we went to Jordan, our friend would pick us up so we could have some fellowship together. The Lord's presence was always wonderfully real as we visited, studied and prayed together.

Not long after our departure from the Near East, Mr. T discovered he had terminal cancer. Although he sought treatment in England, he was no better. He eventually returned to Jordan where he died.

Part VII

The World:
Full Circle

*These are the words of him who is holy
and true, who holds the key of David.
What he opens no one can shut, and
what he shuts no one can open.
(Revelation 3:7)*

22

The End . . . the Beginning

(Miriam)

I'll ride in the leading taxi and the rest of you can follow." It was time for us to leave on furlough. Actually it was time for us to retire from overseas missionary service.

We had grown to love Lebanon so much. Now, on this day, because of fighting on the main road to the airport, one of the young men who knew the area well was volunteering to take us there by a back way.

We hastily boarded the cars and he led us through a maze of narrow side streets until we finally arrived at the airport.

The parting was difficult. There were tears, many tears. Some of these dear friends who were gathered at the airport to see us off had come to know Christ during the last 15 years. We had prayed together, wept together, struggled together through times of uncertainty and danger. Now we were leaving them, not knowing what the future would hold for them or for us.

Joy Dagher had become my dearest friend. We tearfully said goodbye to each other. She stuffed an envelope into my hand and whispered, "Read it when you get on the plane."

We prolonged as long as we could our walk to the airport bus which would take us across the tarmac to the waiting plane. Our hearts were heavy, our vision blurred.

Once on the plane we sank into our assigned seats and the plane took off. It didn't take me long to open Joy's letter. I read it through misty eyes. My heart was so touched with her expressions of love and appreciation.

Retired! Do you like that word? I don't. To me, the connotation of the word "retired" is "ceasing from former activity." It sounds so final.

One day, not long after arriving home and still having difficulty accepting our new retired status, we heard a message on the radio. Although I do not remember the exact words, the thoughts remain:

Retirement is not only an end, it is also a beginning. With God there is no ending. The end of everything marks the beginning of something new.

> Life is full of endings and beginnings. The end of one year brings the beginning of a new one. Events of yesterday are history. Events of tomorrow require a prophetic word. We don't have to worry about tomorrow. Christ who is our life will walk with us all the way.

Some people drag their yesterday into their today, marring its beauty and causing them to miss the present opportunities. Leave yesterday where it belongs. Live today to its fullest for God.

It was a message of comfort and encouragement to two aching hearts.

Now, living here in the United States, there are new opportunities, new challenges. We are enjoying the new beginnings—each new day, each new year. Our testimony is that 57 years of service to Christ and His Church affirm that God is faithful and that He strengthens and empowers those who minister in His name. He confirms His Word. And signs follow.

We expect no less for today . . . nor for tomorrow.

23

The Mission Field Comes to Us

(Miriam)

March of 1990 marked the centennial celebration of the work of The Christian and Missionary Alliance in the Near East. I could hardly believe it was going to be possible for Harry and me to participate.

It was important to me to go. I had so many memories of my early years spent there. Our Breaden family of five had gone to that area of the world in 1923—just 33 years after the first Alliance missionaries had blazed the trail—to work in the land where Jesus was born. My parents' burden was to reach the people with the gospel of Jesus Christ.

The area is known as The Holy Land where so much of biblical history unfolds—the land where Jesus walked and taught, where He died for the sins of the world and where He rose for our justification. Yet so very few there really know Christ as Savior and Lord.

There were many struggles in those days. The missionaries endured much hardship. I was young, but I was aware of their discouragement. I had lived in the Mission house at the hub of missionary activity. I had watched converts struggle with threats of imprisonment by authorities. I had seen others deal with rejection by their family. Even though progress was slow, God faithfully worked behind the scenes to build up the body of believers.

The celebration in Amman was fantastic! Who could have foreseen such jubilation? A triple celebration—the Centennial Festival, the dedication of the newly built edifice at the Second Circle and the ordination of Yousef Hashweh who was succeeding his pastor-father who had died the previous year.

On Monday we boarded the Centennial bus in Amman and followed the road past the Dead Sea, across the Jordan River and into Israel. We toured Galilee for two days before going to Jerusalem.

I was so anxious to see Jerusalem again! I was going back home—to the Alliance headquarters at No. 50 Prophet Street in Jerusalem. On the city map the imposing stone structure is a landmark—a monument to the vision, faith and sacrifice of The Christian and Missionary Alliance over the past century. A miracle!

It is easy for travelers to locate Sharek-el-Nebi (Arabic for Prophet Street). The building is made of hand-cut stone. It has withstood earthquakes and the ravages of war.

It was just as I remembered it—nothing had been changed in the surrounding area except the German consulate next door. I was told it had been severely damaged during fighting and had to be dismantled.

Our building had been freshly sandblasted on the outside and repainted on the inside. Everything looked so fresh and new. It was magnificent! In the upper, larger sanctuary banners were stretched from side to side. The wooden floor was polished. The baptistry was still there. During the program I stood on it to give a short speech about my memories of past experiences as a child. I was the oldest participant representing those years.

In the lower auditorium posters and displays lined the walls. There were refreshments of punch and pieces of decorated celebration cakes—scores of them. The Mission offices, guest home, apartment for the host and hostess and the large living room area were open for viewing. The room Marjorie and I had occupied as young school girls was much as I had remembered it—Room 5 on the second floor.

The speeches, the drama, the music—all contributed to a wonderful celebration, leaving us with overflowing hearts for God's bountiful provisions.

(Harry)

Since our forced departure from Cambodia over 20 years ago, nearly a half million Cambodian citizens have been scattered like leaves in the wind across the continents of the world.

Today, in the United States alone, there are approximately 150,000 Cambodians. The mission field has come to us.

Now, after retiral, we find ourselves back to our original commitment and responsibility. Our Cambodian ministry reaches from Massachusetts to Minnesota, from the Carolinas to California. We have also had the privilege of ministering to Cambodian refugees in France, Switzerland, Thailand and Australia.

In 1990, Miriam and I went to Philadelphia. She was to speak at a rally for the Alliance Women at the Cambodian Church there. The president, Moury Om, gave us her home address where she lived with her mother.

We rang the bell and after some time a gracious, elderly lady opened the door. We introduced ourselves. Moury wasn't home but Yea'a Om, Moury's mother, greeted us with sincere warmth.

"Lok, I know you!" exclaimed the smiling woman.

Miriam and I looked at each other. We had absolutely no recollection of ever having met her, but she insisted that she knew me. She had seen us in Cambodia, she said.

Leading us through a furnitureless room, the woman motioned us into the dining room where there was a round table and four straight chairs.

"When I was just nine years old," she began, "I stood outside your meeting place in Kompong Cham. Your church was right across from the public market. I heard you play your horn and I listened to the Cambodian pastor talk about Jesus. One of my mother's best friends was always in your meetings. They had previously gone to the Buddhist temple together, but when she turned to the 'Jesus Way' she would no longer go to the temple.

That made my mother angry.

"During the holocaust in Cambodia, I managed to flee to Thailand with my three children. We lived as refugees there until we were sent to the Philippines and on to the United States. In this last refugee camp we heard the gospel and my children all accepted Christ as their Savior. My heart continued to be rebellious, but I surrendered to Christ later in America.

"My son, Samuel, is a pastor in California. My younger daughter is attending Nyack College and my older daughter, Moury, is the Alliance Women's leader for our area.

"I used to hate you, but now I love you. My life's ambition is to minister to those who give their lives in the ministry of the gospel of Christ."

Our ambition is similar to that of Yea'a Om's—we want to minister to the Cambodian mission field at our door. The mission field has come to us!

It is not the end. It is a new beginning!

24

Our Children, Too

*Our children too shall serve him, for they
shall hear from us about the wonders of
the Lord. (Psalm 22:30, TLB)*

You have already met each of our children—
Don, Janice and Judith. But now, let us tell
you the rest of the story.

Donald McCartney Taylor

Don was born in Norfolk, Virginia, before we
went to the field. As you have already read, Don
was two years old when his internment camp experience began in the Philippines.

Don accepted Christ as his Savior in children's
meetings held at Beulah Beach, Ohio, where we
spent part of our two-year rehabilitation after
World War II.

As with all of our children, Don attended Dalat
School in Vietnam, a two-day journey from our station in Kompong Cham, Cambodia.

Back at Beulah Beach for summer work after
graduation from high school, Don dedicated his
life to God for missionary service. This commit-

ment took him to Nyack College in the fall of 1955. Between his junior and senior year at Nyack, Don and Janet (Lithgow) were married.

After graduation, he became assistant pastor at Tabernacle Church, in Norfolk, Virginia, the same city where we began our ministry before going to the field. After one year, they transferred to Meadville, Pennsylvania, for an internship program in preparation for their appointment to Cambodia.

Don and Janet were in Cambodia for only one term before the shocking news came that missionary visas would not be renewed. In Don's own words, "The happiest years of my ministry were in Cambodia."

Their new assignment was Thailand. They had just completed language study and proceeded to Surin, their new station, when Don came down with an ear infection. The local doctors attempted to treat him. The injection Don received threw him unconscious to the floor. Now, more than 15 years later, the doctors are still puzzled by the lingering aftereffects of the treatment.

Don and Janet settled in Johnson City, New York, where they helped initiate a new program under the auspices of the local Alliance Church—a ministry to Laotian refugees.

Don and Janet have three children—Kevin, Karen and Keith.

Janice Allaine Taylor Kropp

Janice, as our readers already know, was born in the Philippines. She spent the first three years of her life in a Japanese concentration camp.

Janice also attended Dalat School and later high

school in Florida and Virginia. At Nyack College she continued to prepare for her future. It was there that she met and married Richard Kropp.

After graduation the Kropps were assigned as missionaries to Japan, where they are in their fifth term of service. Dick is field director for Japan.

Dick and Janice have four sons: Karl (married to Vicki), Todd, Alan and Donn.

Judith Esther Taylor Reitz

Judith, our third child, was named after the two women who gave Miriam their vitamin pills in the internment camp.

Judy, like the others, attended Dalat School where she accepted Christ as her Savior at one of the many youth activities. Judy chose as her life verse: "Trust in the LORD with all your heart and lean not on your own understanding; in all your ways acknowledge him and he will make your paths straight" (Proverbs 3:5–6). She says, "There were many things in my life I didn't understand, but it was my goal to trust my Lord and acknowledge His ways."

Following the family tradition, Judy graduated from Nyack College. In 1967, she married George Reitz. After graduating from Bethel Seminary, George accepted a pastorate in Johnson City.

Then, in the late '70s, God took George and Judy to Brooklyn, New York, where they planted and pastored Christ's Community Church. One of their outreaches has been to the Cambodian refugees living in the area. A church has been organized with a Cambodian pastor.

George was recently appointed director of urban

ministries for the Metropolitan District of The
Christian and Missionary Alliance.

They have two sons—Scott and Kristofer.

25

And to Baghdad

The Karentina Alliance Church in Beirut has a thrilling new ministry—in Baghdad, right under the nose of Saddam Hussein!

Sami Dagher, pastor of the Karentina Church, received a burden from the Lord for the people of Iraq. A specialist in the hotel and restaurant business, Sami devised a plan to open up a restaurant in Baghdad. Zadan, a convert of Sami's and one of the top restaurant chefs in Beirut, encouraged this new venture.

Finding himself unemployed due to the strife in Lebanon, Zadan began to work with Sami on plans to execute their project. The plan included sending several zealous young men with Zadan to work and witness for Christ in Iraq.

Then came Desert Shield followed by Desert Storm. But Sami's vision did not fade in the face of the carnage and destruction of the war. Rather, the war served to open doors to take the gospel to the people of Iraq.

One Sunday, Sami announced to the Karentina Church that he needed four young men who were fully committed to Christ to take up the challenge. They were to have no marital ties or interests in Lebanon. They were to be willing to spend the rest of their lives serving Christ in Iraq.

Four men stepped forward—Fadi, Charles, Elias and George. (Hythan later replaced Fadi.)

The guns of war in Iraq were hardly cool when Sami traveled to Baghdad to seek official permission to carry out his new program. The restaurant venture was no longer needed as an opening. Permission for a relief project was immediately granted. The project became known as "Bread for the Starving"—bread for the body and bread for the soul.

The four young volunteers supervised the distribution of food, clothing and medicine supplied by CAMA Services and other relief organizations. They also witnessed openly for Christ in cooperation with the Evangelical Church of Baghdad. This bold venture helped the Baghdad congregation grow in spiritual vitality and numbers. About 60,000 people, plus 6,000 orphans, received material help and 1,000 Bibles were distributed.

This ministry did not go unnoticed. The Ministry of Religious Affairs sent a letter of appreciation to the Evangelical Church in Baghdad and the Ministry of Labor and Social Affairs expressed gratitude to the Karentina Church in Beirut.

Sami took the opportunity to explain his motivation for the project to the minister in charge. He recounted the events of his own personal conversion to Christ. And then he added, "Since my conversion, I love instead of hate. We come here to

Iraq with food, clothing and medicine to alleviate the physical needs of the starving. We also bring the Word of God to meet the heart needs of your people. Jesus gives eternal life to all who will believe."

During the second phase of the project, Sami sent a letter to Saddam Hussein, once again giving his personal testimony and sharing with Mr. Hussein the burden of the Karentina Church to show the love of Christ to the people of Iraq. This so impressed Saddam that he had the letter printed on the front page of leading Iraqi newspapers. As a result he also permitted the *Jesus* film to be shown by Campus Crusade on prime time television throughout the country.

And the sequel to this story? Now there is an outreach to the Kurds of northern Iraq who fled into Syria during the war. Sami was given permission to supply those previously untouched, poverty-stricken Kurdish refugees with food, supplies and Bibles.

And the doors for evangelical witness continue to open ever wider.

Afterword

Glancing over our shoulders at the past 57 years of ministry in serving the Lord Jesus Christ, our hearts are deeply aware of His grace and mercy. We have been conscious that our Lord has not been looking for great people, but rather, for those who believe He is great.

In our many weaknesses and shortcomings we have marveled at His faithfulness to His Word: "I will never leave you or forsake you."

All praise and honor go to our Lord and Savior, Jesus Christ!